CONVERSATIONS WITH COMPANIONS

MASTERING COMMUNICATION WITH YOUR PETS

JOANNE YEOH

ACCLAIM FOR CONVERSATIONS WITH COMPANIONS: MASTERING COMMUNICATION WITH YOUR PETS

I love this book! In a thoughtful, carefully crafted manner, Joanne gives excellent strategies to communicate with your beloved animal companions. And it works! While reading, I kept jumping up to embrace Kyler and Bella (our two dogs). I could 'hear' their voices and feel the depth of their love in a much deeper way than before. Our cat Muse 'told' me she wanted to be able to look out the window, so I immediately ordered a cat tree for her. I think she will love it! What a wonderful, heartfelt book! Highly recommended.

Denise Linn,
author Sacred Space

Is communicating with our own pets harder than with other people's pets? Only if we make it harder! Professional Animal Communicator, Joanne Yeoh, wants us all to succeed in communicating with the animals that mean the most to us – our pets. In *Conversations with Companions: Mastering Communication with your Pets*, Joanne offers inspiring stories and practical exercises to expand our minds, and our animal communication tool kits, to help us have the best relationships with our pets that we can. What a gift! With this book, Joanne will help you master animal communication with your pets, too!

Dr. Cara Gubbins,
Professional Animal Communicator,
author and founder of the Animal Communicator Academy

This ground-breaking, honest and mind-expanding book will help you elevate your connection with your pets to a whole new level. The practical steps and stories guide you to feel and embody a new way of experiencing and being with all animals you encounter in your life.

Rachel Knott,
founder of My Animal Matters Ltd,
MA (LINT) Dip IAZ

Joanne's book is refreshing in its accessibility. Rather than adding to the mystical stereotype of animal communication, her inclusive language and explanations encourage us all to think in more depth about our interactions and communications and how we might seek to develop them further. Whether or not this book inspires you to develop your own abilities, as a minimum, it creates a desire for animal lovers to look with greater compassion and understanding at why the pets we share our lives with may be acting the way they do – and that can only be a good thing, right?

Dr. Zoë Freedman,
MChiro PGCert MSc DC

As a professional pet sitter, I found this book a 'must read' for anyone wanting to go above and beyond to ensure the pets in their care have their every need met. Pet parents will find this book a life-changing step towards discovering the secrets of their pets' inner thoughts, so working together, they can make their brief lives all the more fulfilling.

Louisa Wheeler,
founder of Somerset Cat Sitting

I am touched that Joanne's book is dedicated to the memory of my sister, Isabelle. Guided by Joanne's compassionate hand, we each find our animal communication style and deepen our relationships with the pets we love. Her communication exercises help us return to our hearts. From there, we open to new and greater possibilities – for ourselves and the animals we love.

Arleen Hannich,
MA, CCM (Chief Cat Minion)

I can't even find the words to describe the difference you've made, Joanne, to me and the many domestic and feral animals for whom I provide healing energy. While I've always known animals can communicate with us, it had seemed an intuitive energy exchange between me and them, and only for healing.

What an exciting new world opened to me through your patient guidance and techniques after taking your classes and now reading your book. Experiencing the world of sights, sounds, smells, tastes and feelings – not to mention experiencing their wise awareness – has been the most rewarding experience of my life. Not only have your teachings deepened my communication to find out information to heal the wild animals, and given me a more rounded and mutual relationship with my own pets, it has deepened my spiritual acceptance of, compassion for, and honouring of all life forms, and confirmed that we all are equals in Oneness.

You have taught me that intuition is communication with any living being, transcending and including our normal communication language with other beings, human or otherwise. All I can say is wow, and thank you.

Jeanni McBride,
Clinical Psychologist

I love that all the stories allowed me to connect and relate so easily to the relationships I have with our two dogs. Joanne's simple and straightforward instructions and experience then gave me the route to building a much closer bond with them both.

Imagine if you'd had this information much earlier in your relationship with your pet family, and how amazing that would be for you all and your futures together! A must for any animal guardian's toolkit.

Claire Walker,
founder and publisher of Intuitive You

Until I experienced it, I wondered if animal communication was a 'real thing'. Yes – it sure is! My life changed forever as I used the skills in my work with hundreds of dogs, and at home with my own dogs. And it is a skill – one that can be taught and is available to everyone, as long as you're prepared to practise and delve deeper into a world that has been hidden in plain sight.

Joanne's beautifully written and accessible book teaches you how to listen to animals on a different frequency. Like turning a dial on a radio, we can gain a higher perspective not just of them, but of ourselves and our own potential. Learn how to open the door for yourself and unlock the magic that has always been there, just waiting to be discovered.

Natalie Lenton,
owner and director of Canine Massage Therapy Centre,
author of Canine Massage in 3 Easy Steps (DVD).

CONVERSATIONS WITH COMPANIONS: MASTERING COMMUNICATION WITH YOUR PETS

Deep Pacific Press
117 E 37th Street #580
Loveland, CO 80538

Deep
Pacific
Press

DeepPacificPress.com

ISBN 978-1-956108-06-4 (paperback)
ISBN 978-1-956108-07-1 (eBook)

Interior Design by Quantum Shift Media
Cover Design by Fancy Gecko

animalcommunicationinsights.com
info@animalcommunicationinsights.com

Disclaimer

The information shared in this book is for educational and informational purposes only and is not intended to be viewed as medical or mental health advice. It is not designed to be a substitute for professional advice from your veterinarian, physician, therapist, attorney, accountant or any other health care practitioner or licensed professional. The Publisher and the Author do not make any guarantees as to the effectiveness of any of the techniques, suggestions, tips, ideas or strategies shared in this book as each situation differs. The Publisher and Author shall neither have liability nor responsibility with respect to any direct or indirect loss or damage caused or alleged by the information shared in this book related to your health, life or business or any other aspect of your situation. It is your responsibility to do your own due diligence and use your own judgement when applying any techniques or situations mentioned in or through this book. References to some persons or situations in this book are fictional, though they may be based on real life situations. Written permission has been obtained to share the identity of any real individual named in this book. Any citations or sources of information from other organisations or websites are not endorsements of the information or content the website or organisation provides or recommendations it may make. Please be aware that any websites or references that were available during publication may not be available in the future.

Dedication

I dedicate this book to the memory of Isabelle Hannich. Her guidance and belief in me shaped the way I encourage loving pet parents to learn animal communication so they can understand their companions by communicating in their shared language.

Though my time with Isabelle was short, the transformation she evoked in me will last all my days.

Contents

Foreword
JOSH COEN

You know that excitement and anticipation you feel when a sequel to your favourite movie comes out? The continuation of a beloved story or adventure filled with familiar, treasured characters is not only thrilling, but comforting. For me, this book is like that sequel – a brand new way to experience the magic of Joanne Yeoh and her special approach to teaching animal communication. It's an approach I grew to know and love about three years into my own animal communication quest – and with a front row VIP seat to all the action.

You see, my pre-Joanne journey to learning this skill began like so many others report. I took an online course, made very little headway with the teacher's techniques, felt intimidated by the successes of the more advanced students, and desperately wondered why I couldn't get this to work for me. At the end, I had more knowledge, but not much more success at animal communication. And I really put in the time and work!

Was I just not cut out for this? Did I lack the 'gifts' or talents necessary? Was I doing something wrong or blocking my own progress in some way? It felt really bad, but I knew I was not alone. Almost every one of the fifty students taking that course was having the same experience, and I knew upon completion, most of them would scatter to the wind, along with their dreams of talking with animals. I was determined that wasn't going to be me – and if I could help it, it wouldn't be the rest of the world's aspiring animal communicators either.

Over the next five years, I built and ran Speak! Good Human, the world's largest cost-free animal communication practice site, filled with teacher wisdom, student support, inspiring stories, lots of techniques to try, and hundreds of animals to talk with – including access to their people for feedback on those conversations. Thousands of floundering students worldwide made their way to Speak! Good Human to find hope and a way forward.

As a learner myself, and from my position at the helm of this venture, I knew what they were going through, what challenges they faced and insecurities they battled. I also knew what I wished had been part of that original online course – a way to practise that built confidence, rather than eroding it. Knowing everyone has a unique path to learning this skill, my goal was to offer a plethora of perspectives, approaches and techniques so everyone would be sure to find what worked for them. My outside-the-box thinking, thanks to a long career in advertising, helped fuel so many of those creative ideas. It's also why I immediately clicked with Joanne's innovative teaching style when we first crossed paths through the Speak! project.

Joanne also wasn't interested in the same standard processes and techniques you find elsewhere in this field. She was more interested in bursting those myths and achieving results. Not only did Joanne take me up on my standing offer to any teacher who wanted an online practice space for their students – she did more with that space than any other instructor. With her personal approach to every learner and her never-ending, creative ideas, Joanne helped them overcome blocks, find their own styles, build confidence and blossom into the animal communicators she knew they were.

Joanne is the teacher I wish I'd had from the beginning! This is the teacher I wish everyone had from the beginning, and I'm honoured that so many did through their Speak! connection.

If you're one of them, you share my excitement at this 'Joanne sequel' and know why it is so special. But if this is your first introduction to her, you are in a position just as exciting, because you don't have to wait for that sequel. You can just dive in right now ... and what you'll discover is an animal communication book unlike any other. It's not a traditional 'what is' or 'how to' manual, but a unique way to explore what's possible in communicating with the animals in your life. And just like real-life Joanne, it will build your confidence with every page turn, whether you're a beginner or well into your animal communication training.

At its heart, you'll find a dozen first-hand stories that address one of the biggest myths in this field head-on – that it's harder to communicate with your own animal than with others. In each vignette, you'll hear directly from the animal, the animal's person, and from Joanne as moderator and guide. Through their creative, personalised problem-solving, you'll see how they went from communication trouble to communication success, enabling a much deeper, more fulfilling relationship. The animal felt heard, and their person learned how to tailor their communication style to strengthen their bond. And you, the reader, get an inside look into how to expand your thinking when approaching your own animal communication challenges at home.

In addition to these perspective-changing stories, Joanne's trademark confidence-boosting style gently leads you forward with lots of no-stress exercises, tips, ideas and other guidance throughout. It's all designed to help you uncover your animal's unique perspectives, preferences and process so you can master this shared language and forge the kind of understanding and connection between you that most only dream about.

True to my own belief and the premise I set forth at Speak! Good Human, *Conversations with Companions: Mastering Communication with your Pets* leaves no doubt that everyone can learn this skill, it just takes finding your own path to get there. With Joanne as your guide, not only will you never go wrong, but you'll always go right.

Wishing you and the animals in your life many magical moments together.

Josh

Josh Coen
Speak! Good Human
talktoanimals.weebly.com

Invitation

This book is for all who believe pets have feelings and are important members of the family. Through learning how to communicate with your pet, you'll discover what they can tell you, transforming the relationship you share!

This book is not a training manual, nor does it claim to fix your pet's problems. Communicating with your pet is not so you can tell them what to do, nor should you assume they will obey you just because they can hear and understand you.

Over the years, my pets have taught me that animal communication is about learning their language – not me talking to them in human language and expecting them to understand the details of what I'm saying.

I hope to inspire you to see your pets as 'more than just a pet' and to learn the language of animals and connect with their wisdom. Each story in this book gives an example of how creative communications from pets are. They are so diverse there's a story for everyone to relate to, detailing the experiences each communicator has had with their own animal communication learning, plus how they value communication with their own pet as a way to strengthen and improve their bond.

Many of the people I've worked with have found that once they learned how to speak their pet's language (asking questions in the way their pet understands and being able to receive the answers), they noticed a dramatic improvement in their pet's behaviour and emotional state. This can be attributed to them now having the awareness and insight to know how to meet their pet's specific needs, as described by their pet.

Communication with an animal is a two-way conversation, just as it is with humans. It is absolutely 100% guaranteed that your pets want you to learn their language, and they'll even help you! Pet parents tell me they worry their pets may get impatient with them or think they're being slow to learn when they first attempt to converse in their pet's language. I assure you that is absolutely not true, and you know it too, because your pets are unconditionally loving. They want the best for you and for themselves, and there is no reason they wouldn't want you to learn their language, because it will enhance your relationship with them.

The teaching elements of this book will take you through the foundations of communicating with your pets and will leave you excited about how much more love and fun you can experience with your treasured companions. It is a process that will require you to be open with your experiences and trust in yourself. The example exercises (reflections) can be applied to all domestic pets.

I urge you to approach *Conversations with Companions: Mastering Communication with your Pets* with a sense of curiosity and fun!

To sign up to my free *Roadmap To Mastering Animal Communication with your Pet,* type this address below into your web browser: animalcommunicationinsights.com/roadmap/

The Miracle

My wish is for this book to inspire you to want to learn to communicate with your pets without the fear of getting it wrong, and to believe that you have within you the natural ability to talk with and listen to your pets!

The two most popular questions I hear from pet owners are 'Is my pet happy?' and 'What more can I do to make my pet's life better?' Often, they wish their pet could talk so they could understand them better, especially when they struggle with behavioural problems or their pet is in emotional distress. They know how to gauge what their pets are feeling by observing their body language and second-guessing the verbal responses, but this doesn't always give the full picture of what their pet is truly experiencing.

I remember when I first started exploring communicating with my dog, Donny. I'd ask simple questions, such as 'What is your favourite toy?' Then my mind would come up with the answer, 'Ball'. I already knew that about him, so how would I know for sure he had actually communicated that to me?

I'd also ask 'How are you feeling? Are you okay? Is there anything you want to tell me?' Then my mind would draw a blank. Nothing would come to me. It was as if I'd entered a dark room. Sometimes I felt like I was hitting a brick wall. I couldn't work out how to get past it and kept thinking I was doing it wrong. Why had the ability been there when I watched a film of an animal communicator helping an animal – I just tried it, without really knowing what I was doing, yet Donny could communicate with me at that point. Then when I started learning animal communication more formally and followed the steps, the results seemed to be hit and miss. To me this was ironic. I came across animal communication *because* of my own pets, something that was going on with them, something that troubled me and made me curious.

As the story unfolds about my work as an animal communicator, you'll see how, time and time again, I came across a common problem – pet owners, as well as trained animal communicators, would tell me they found communicating with their own pets more difficult than with other people's pets. Although most of the time they believed their pets could understand what they were saying, they were never sure they could hear their pets' answers.

And so, a simple idea ensued. I decided to gather twelve animal communicators from my online Community Group and ask what they found challenging about communicating with their own pets. More than that, I would then communicate with their pets to ask them directly how their communications together could be improved and made easier. What I wanted to know was *do their pets agree with the belief that communicating with one's own pets was difficult?*

As these communications took place with the dogs, cats, a horse and a turtle, the stories began to form as uniquely as each individual pet. The communicators gave their account of how their pet came into their life, their own path to discovering animal communication and the struggle they had communicating with their own pet. In turn, their pet would relay to me what their thoughts and feelings were towards their parent and give suggestions and make requests for how they would like their communication channels to be improved. Each communication ends with what the pet wanted to say, followed by a short exercise for you to try.

CHAPTER 1

Start with Your Pets
Opening up the Discussion

Starting out learning animal communication, I didn't come across many teachings for communicating with your own pets. Mostly, it was practising and working with other people's pets. In fact, it was widely accepted that communicating with your own pets is more difficult because you can be too close to them, too emotionally connected, so you may not get good results. I often heard other animal communicators say, '*Oh, I can communicate with other people's pets, but when it comes to mine, I can't do it or it's really difficult.*'

Generally, consensus in the animal communication community seems to regard communicating with your own pets to be harder.

We're also taught to believe:

- It's best to start from a blank canvas and not have any prior information about the pet.
- It's better to communicate with other people's pets first so you can receive feedback from the pet's person.
- It's advisable not to allow your emotions to get in the way which can influence the connection when communicating.

In many ways, this book opens up the discussion that it is *not* more difficult to communicate with your own pets, but it is *different* compared to communicating with other people's pets.

What happens when you start learning animal communication with your own pets first?

Your pets will be thrilled and delighted! After all, it's likely you became interested in animal communication because you wanted to communicate with them. Your pets are always available to practise with. Creating daily opportunities to learn together is a fantastic way to strengthen your bond.

I believe practising with your own pets is the best way to gain real and honest feedback for your animal communication learning. Their feedback might be by a change in the way they interact with you or a shift in their behaviour, so you'll know it's real. For example, when I wanted to adopt Ziggi (a cat) into my family of dogs, I communicated with them all about it beforehand. Everything went so smoothly the day they all met. At first, I wondered if maybe it was a coincidence. But I know my dogs. They would usually be stressed and highly excitable in that type of situation, so their response gave me confidence in knowing the communication was real.

CHAPTER 2

Speaking Their Language

Communicating Using the 7 Sensory (Intuitive) Signs

7 Sensory (Intuitive) Signs your pet is using to communicate with you:

1. **Visuals** - Your pet can send you a flash of an image – perhaps colour(s), shape, a scene, an object, and even a 'movie' playing in your mind.
2. **Sounds** - Your pet can share sounds they hear with you. It can start quietly, so when you notice the sound coming to you, ask your pet to increase the volume so you can hear it better.
3. **Smells** - Turn your attention (with your eyes closed) to the area of your nostrils and pause there a while. Do you suddenly get a whiff of a scent or fragrance? Be alert to this, as it may come and go quite quickly as your pet shares scents with you.

4. **Taste** - Bring your awareness to the inside of your mouth as you ask your pet to share the taste of their meal. Are you aware of a subtle change of taste in your mouth? Perhaps you can even detect a certain texture or find yourself salivating – or even experiencing a taste you don't find pleasant!

5. **Emotions** - Your mood can shift and your energy change almost in an instant when connecting with your pet. They're sharing with you how they feel at that moment!

6. **Physical Sensations** - An itch, goosebumps, even tingling, as well as a gentle warmth radiating through your body, are the sensations your pets will communicate to let you know how they are physically experiencing their body.

7. **Knowingness/Experiences/Memories** - It might be an idea or thought that crosses your mind as you ask your pet a question, a memory you recall that you weren't expecting, or even a recollection of a situation you've been through as you connect with your pet.

Do you need to be gifted to communicate with your pets? What if you didn't grow up surrounded by animals and nature? What if right now you don't share your life with a pet, but you had pets in the past, or plan to in the future? Is *Conversations with Companions: Mastering Communication with your Pets* for you too? YES!

CHAPTER 3

How It Began for Me

Transforming Relationships with My Pets

I often experienced 'stories in my head' as a child and referred to them as *Imagined Information*. They would simply pop into my mind. I'd sometimes talk about this to the adults around me, only to realise not many shared my excitement and awe at how my mind would hold these conversations. As I grew older, I dismissed my Imagined Information as unimportant, and certainly not something to be spoken about openly. Forty-plus years later, I became aware that how Imagined Information came to me so easily as a child is how animals actually communicate with me!

I didn't grow up surrounded by animals and nature, and often I wonder how on earth I ended up becoming an animal communicator! My childhood was influenced by those who favoured logic over intuition. I was taught not to believe what the eye couldn't see.

I pursued a career in administration and finance as a result of external pressure to succeed in a mainstream profession. As the years went by, this didn't bring the sense of purpose I had desperately sought throughout my life. I didn't realise then that I needed a connection to 'what the eye couldn't see', in other words, something bigger than me, perhaps even outside of myself – things I couldn't prove existed, yet my senses would connect with. I became drawn to psychology, self-development work, creative arts, religious studies, and even found myself fascinated by the work of clairvoyants, yet I continued to hold a level of scepticism in order to remain loyal to the power of rationale.

In late adulthood, I became more and more disillusioned with the meaning of life, coupled with the stresses of my career, pushing me to start questioning the path my life was taking. Becoming interested in holistic therapies and new age practices, in time I trained and qualified in aromatherapy, kinesiology and hypnotherapy. I left my career in administration and finance in 1996 to start my holistic therapy business, then completed a certified practitioner programme in 2013, Soul Coaching® Oracle Card by Denise Linn, heralding the deepening of my intuitive skills, which I used to help myself and others. Included in the programme was membership to an online community group where I could connect with others and exchange and practice card readings. Then one day, this request from a member was posted:

'Hi everyone. I am about to call an animal communicator for my cat, Kidden. I thought I'd give a shout out here first if someone needs to practice with the cards. You can message me if you prefer. Thank you!'

Isabelle

Within this programme were card reading layout examples, including the 'Animal Companion Spread', a series of seven cards picked with the theme of receiving intuitive guidance to understand your pet. This caught my interest and I responded immediately to Isabelle's message. Up to that point, the majority of requests for card readings were for people, rather than pets, and I was curious how this would work with Kidden the cat. I sent a message to Isabelle saying I'd be happy to practise using the Animal Companion Spread card layout.

Excited about what I would discover, I set time aside to use the Soul Coaching® Oracle Card deck. I picked out the seven cards, focusing on the photograph of Kidden that Isabelle had sent me. This was my preferred way of working, as I trusted I didn't need to be in Kidden's physical presence to connect with her – my Imagined Information and intuition would work together. Although I was using oracle cards to connect intuitively for messages about Kidden, I discovered I was also receiving additional information unrelated to the meaning of the oracle cards. At that point, I hadn't realised that Kidden was communicating directly to me about her personality, describing aspects of her life and sharing about what was troubling her. When I sent Isabelle what I had written down of the 'reading' of Kidden, she replied:

'Thank you, Joanne! A great and accurate reading. The cards never lie, and your interpretations of them were spot on!'

I didn't know Isabelle was an animal communicator. It was a complicated time for her when we connected as she was in remission from cancer. She was beginning to feel stronger and held plans to return to helping others with their spiritual quest. The magical part of our encounter was that we were in different parts of the world, yet Isabelle could send me photos of her cats and I would communicate with them, sending her the information by email.

Isabelle and I corresponded regularly over the next few months. She had eleven cats and I would take it in turn to communicate with every single one of them! Isabelle would share her feedback, and if I received information from any of her cats that I wasn't sure of, she'd explain things in a way that helped me understand their meanings. She became my unofficial mentor.

We had an easy arrangement, whereby I had the opportunity to explore this exciting phenomenon of being able to receive Imagined Information about her cats, and it seemed I had at last found someone who was as interested and excited about it as I was!

A proud moment for me was when Isabelle wrote an update in the Oracle Card community page, telling the members:

'Hi all. I want to give a shout out to a lovely soul, Joanne Yeoh. A few months ago, I asked if anyone was doing animal communication readings and Joanne raised her hand to try. We have been working together ever since! Her readings are very professionally done AND accurate! She is working hard every day to learn more about animal communication, and especially, how to trust her OWN intuition. She's finding her own style and I think that is just fantastic. Way to go, Joanne, and I hope we keep working together!'

Shortly after Isabelle wrote this, she found out her cancer had returned. Within five months of our first contact, she passed away. Upon hearing the news of Isabelle's death, I didn't have anyone to share my loss with who would understand – after all, Isabelle could be regarded as a stranger by many who may not be able to appreciate the impact she had on me.

Isabelle gave me the gift of listening to my Imagined Information, and she believed in me. I decided to turn my grief into a plan of action and vowed to make Isabelle proud of me. I fearlessly stepped forward on my own and began to explore the work of renowned animal communicators to further my learning. I read books, watched tutorial videos and attended seminars. My experiences while formally studying animal communication were a far cry from the personalised and insightful guidance I'd received from Isabelle.

Although there was no doubt in my mind that animal communication was real, I constantly doubted I could do it. It seemed each time I was asked to communicate with someone's pet, my initial enthusiasm would quickly give way to the sheer nervousness I felt about getting things wrong.

What if I passed on the information to the pet's parent, only for them to tell me it didn't make sense or was incorrect? I felt like I was risking my reputation, and the fear of being ridiculed for believing I had the 'gift' of being able to talk to animals would make me procrastinate, and even avoid setting time aside for communication. What if I found out I couldn't do this? I could be the exception to the rule that 'animal communication is naturally within us' and the belief that 'everyone can do this'.

My thoughts then returned to when Isabelle was guiding me. I never felt afraid when I connected with her cats and shared their communications with her. Why was that? I realised that with Isabelle I could be myself. I wasn't trying to be like anyone else, nor comparing myself with other communicators. I had the freedom of sharing my experience of the communications without the worry of getting it wrong or thinking Isabelle would say I was crazy. Although Isabelle knew her cats well and her relationship with them was good, she was also open to finding out what her cats needed to say, and she trusted me.

So that was it! I began to understand that my struggle was not about whether I could communicate with animals or not, but that comparing myself with other communicators resulted in me thinking I wasn't good enough. I knew then I needed to find my own style and be comfortable with the way I worked.

This new-found determination spurred me to move forward, so I made a goal to contact 100 pet parents and offer to practise on their pets as case studies. I wanted personal evidence that I could communicate with other people's pets – and do it in my own style. Within six months I had exceeded my goal! The results both astonished and excited me. This was real!

From the case studies, I received further referrals. In time, my services were in demand. I decided to dedicate my life's work to helping pet parents and their companions and founded my business, Animal Communication Insights. In the years since, my family of pets has grown, from my first dog Donny, to Mitch, Ziggi and Mhyah.

Animal communication has transformed my relationship with my pets – and can do the same for you.

CHAPTER 4

My Pets Have Been My Best Teachers

Recognising Their Personal Communication Style

I'll always remember the day I had run out of options to find a cure for my male Bichon dog, Donny. He was exhibiting an ongoing behaviour that brought out my frustration and helplessness. The constant battle to stop him from incessantly chewing and over-licking his paws meant keeping watch almost 24/7. Over three years our relationship became a battleground – with me shouting at him to stop, blaming him for not doing as he was told, and starting to regard him as a problem. Then the guilt would set in, as my behaviours highlighted my helplessness in not knowing how to help him. I had advice coming at me from all angles, but having tried it all, nothing worked long term.

One day I stumbled upon a short film that told the story of an animal communicator demonstrating how she helped an animal who was struggling to settle in its new environment. Something about the film resonated with me deeply, the way the communicator listened to the animal, rather than questioning and seeking to fix the animal. What struck me was how the connection between the two of them was so respectful. Although the communicator was brought in to help the animal, she didn't see herself as more important or more knowledgeable. Rather, she took the time simply to *be* with the animal, as opposed to *doing*, and in that quiet space the animal could confide in her how he was feeling.

From watching the film, I realised I'd never once asked Donny how he felt, nor given him time and space to tell me what was on his mind. In all honesty, it had never occurred to me he could tell me in a way I would understand, which was why I hadn't tried it before. I tentatively mimicked what the animal communicator in the film did, and to my surprise, I heard Donny say, 'My back hurts.' The information came through simply and clearly. It was as if he sent the words into my mind so I could understand them. And at the same time, I remember feeling a subtle physical sensation along my lower back. In that moment too, I experienced a 'gut feeling' and knew I was not imagining it.

I asked Donny to continue, to tell me what else was on his mind, and told him I was sorry I hadn't given him a chance to communicate with me. I was so busy getting stressed out about how his behaviour impacted on me that I hadn't taken the time to listen to him. We continued for a while longer as he shared more about his situation and what he needed from me. I knew it was important to take notice of this information. The outcome blew me away, as Donny literally stopped chewing and licking his paws after three days, when I focused on relieving his back pain and made other necessary changes he said he needed.

My relationship with Donny transformed. From that day, I've been able to speak *his* language. Before that I could only surmise, speak for him, talk about him, label him, second guess what he wanted and needed, and even dismiss what was important to him. I not only found the solution needed to alleviate Donny's chronic condition, but the direction of my life took a different path. Because of Donny, my own journey began and I dedicated my life to working as an animal communicator.

And bang! Ziggi, my male cat, saw his life explode in front of his very eyes. At just two years old, he was involved in a traumatic attack that tore through his abdominal muscle tissues. The veterinary surgeon who operated on Ziggi used the term 'shredded' to describe what he faced when he opened him up. The stitches could barely hold his wound together.

Not one medical opinion held out any hope of him surviving. I prepared myself for the worst as I listened to the advice that it would be kinder to have him euthanised. When it came to making that final decision, I suddenly heard this still small voice calling out to me, 'I want to come home. Let me come home. I am not ready to die.' And I just knew it was Ziggi.

I listened as intently as I could.

Ziggi's voice cut through the noise of my doubts and fearful thoughts. He did a good job getting through to me, as I chose to go against the strong advice around me. Instead, I fought for him and took him home amidst criticism, judgement, and even pity from a few. The general opinion was that I was keeping Ziggi alive for my own needs, that I was in denial of the fact he would not survive, let alone be made well again. Yet I could not shake off that voice, which kept repeating he wanted to come home.

I'd experienced nothing like that, yet I instinctively knew I had to give Ziggi time to show me whether what I heard him say was true. Even though he was leaking urine and had pressure sores from being unable to walk or sit up, I took him home to nurse him day and night. Many times, I agonised over whether I'd done the right thing, but the moment that thought came into my mind, I would hear him say, 'I am not ready to die.' And I could see it in his eyes – the determination not to give up. Ziggi knew he had to convince me to keep strong, to believe in him.

Miraculously, within three months of being home, and having started acupuncture treatment, Ziggi started to make efforts to sit up! Slowly but surely, I watched his recovery as he also regained bladder control. A further month on, Ziggi wobbled his way upright, got up on all fours and tentatively began to walk. Each day he got stronger and stronger, until he blew me away when he started to run, albeit with a slight drag in his hind legs. To me, he was whole again!

Ziggi changed the way I viewed an animal's life, in that they have a right to choose whether they are ready to die, or not.

Beautiful Mary, a female rescue crossbreed whom I renamed Mhyah, was found on the streets of Bulgaria at six months old by an organisation who rescued her and brought her to the United Kingdom by road. When I switched on my computer that day and happened to see her photograph on the rescue organisation's website, our eyes locked. Almost immediately, we began to 'converse', as naturally as two new acquaintances would. I told her about myself, my home and my family. She listened. She spoke about her discomfort and anxiety about the journey. I listened. When I closed the computer down, I knew my next move was to make enquiries to adopt her.

Within four weeks, Mhyah entered my life and began a new chapter for herself with Donny, Mitch and Ziggi. I remember being so excited, thinking of all the wonderful things I could give to her and introduce her to. Her excitement matched mine, and all appeared well until two weeks had passed. Mhyah started to be destructive in the house, chewing items, and at times she would soil indoors. Outdoors became a bigger challenge and she would not come back when called when I let her off the lead. In fact, she would disappear. Boy, could she run fast! When I tracked her down, it was a merry dance to get her back on the lead.

I soon became frustrated, which led me into more controlling behaviours and turning to training and behaviour books and implementing them to the ninth degree. The fun and excitement of Mhyah coming to join me began to wane, a sign I had forgotten to listen to her, to find out how she was feeling and what was going on for her.

One day, she got so fed up with my training regime that she ran from me, and when I chased her, she got herself onto the road. Mhyah stood in the middle of the road and stared back at me, as if to say, 'This is not what I am meant to be. This is not who I am. This is not the life I want.' Slowly edging towards her, my mind panicked – a car could speed along at any moment and there she was, standing right in the middle of the road. As I heard her tell me she was unhappy, my heart broke. We made a pact there and then. I said I would listen to her more and trust that she would choose what was right for her. In the second I said that, Mhyah came towards me, let me put the lead on her, and we walked back home.

Since then, Mhyah and I have become close companions. She is my protector, my friend, my daughter. Our bond is deep felt. Our relationship is based on listening to one another.

And here comes my male Pomeranian, Mitch, running in! He greets each day with a level of enthusiasm that reminds me life is to be lived as if each day is your last. He had been consistently doing this for twelve years, until one day he suddenly fell ill. Within an instant he lost his balance and developed a head tilt and nystagmus (irregular jerking eye movements). A vet visit resulted in the instruction to take Mitch urgently to a specialist for a brain scan, as it was suspected a brain tumour could be causing the presenting symptoms.

Mitch communicated that he wanted to stay where he was, without experiencing further stress. Initially I argued with him. How could I risk not getting him urgent treatment? But I knew I needed to listen. For the next five days, Mitch stayed quiet and hardly ate. On the sixth day, this robust little man got up and started to walk without falling over and his appetite returned.

Mitch has always made his own decisions. Even on the day his previous owner had asked me over to her house to discuss the possibility of me adopting Mitch, he'd already decided. When I went to leave, Mitch ran to my car and promptly jumped in! His owner stood back, aghast. She said he'd never done that and was not known to go with people he didn't know. Mitch made it so clear that his previous owner made the final decision to give him up.

Mitch's adoption story was not because he wasn't loved. His needs were not understood, and that showed up in his behaviour – peeing indoors – ruining curtains, bedding and carpets. He would also chase the cats and hump his dog companion, a Sheltie. Let me tell you now, Mitch is a Pomeranian, smaller than the cats and the Sheltie!

With Mitch in my car, on the way home to start his new life, I said to him I was fine if he needed to share his stresses with me, but could he tell me in ways other than the behaviour he'd been using. From the moment Mitch stepped into my home, he never once soiled indoors, and he respected Donny's place in the pack.

Mitch's communication is always simple and to the point. His preference is to use physical body language and verbal cues for everyday requests, and communications when deeper conversations are to be shared.

Each of my pets has their communication story for the way they have helped me to understand what they want to tell me.

I'm often asked how you can be sure it is your pet who is communicating with you, and not something you've made up. In fact, this is probably the biggest stumbling block for pet parents. Is it simply a matter of waiting for answers to come into your mind when you ask your pet a question? And if so, how do you know it's not your own thoughts? And what if the answer you receive when you've asked your pet a question is something you already know about your pet?

What is your pet trying to tell you in those moments they stare at you a certain way? Do you get the feeling they're trying to tell you something, but you just can't work it out? Perhaps your pet is a quiet soul and you wonder whether they need more from you, but you're unsure how to access their answer.

Are you ready to read the first three of the twelve featured pet communication stories to find out what a cat, dog and turtle want to say in relation to the above? Let's go!

CHAPTER 5

Truth

Annette and her
Female Cat, Tasha

'How on earth can I know if what I'm saying to Tasha is getting through?' Annette often asks this question. 'I feel as if I could be talking to myself!'

That's how we can feel when our communications appear to be one-way. Too preoccupied with our own mind, we may miss the cues that signal we are being heard. We may hold insecurities about whether what we're saying is important or interesting enough for another to acknowledge, lacking the confidence that our own voice is worthy. As a result, communications can become strained and what we mean to say cannot be expressed the way we want it to. Thus, we can often feel others talk over us, so we become the silent ones without an advocate. What follows is how Tasha showed Annette there is more than one way to 'speak'.

WHAT ANNETTE HAD TO SAY:

I'm interested in various spiritual practices and had been to see a medium. He told me I was going to be able to look at a dog and know what was wrong with it, and that I'd be able to do this to help other people and their pets. Shocked, I wasn't sure what he meant or how I was supposed to be able to do that. Synchronicity played a part, as I happened to see an advertisement about animal communication, which made me wonder if that was what he meant.

I then spent a year studying animal communication with various courses online. Then a friend who owned a Westie dog told me her dog wouldn't stop barking. She kept saying she might have to give him up, and I remember thinking that if I could communicate with him and find out why he was doing it, then I could help them both. I really wanted to find a solution to stop him from having to go into a rescue. This motivated me to continue looking for other courses to study more, and along the way I joined Joanne's animal communication group.

I have Tasha, my rescue cat, who I find quite strange due to a few behaviours and mannerisms I don't understand. She stares at me so much. I know she's trying to say something to me, but I don't know what it is. I'd just love to know what she's thinking! I talk to Tasha all the time, out loud and in my mind. I'd ask Tasha questions, and although I believed I got the answers, I was never really sure if they were from her or if it was just me answering myself. I was curious what Tasha would say to Joanne about how I can improve my communication with her.

Joanne began by asking Tasha how I could involve her in my conversations. Tasha said that, firstly, she finds it difficult to translate all the human words. She sometimes catches a word here and there and can piece together what I'm saying from that, but usually only with words I use often and she has learnt their meanings.

Tasha mentioned to Joanne that I talk a lot about going to the shops. She was right, because I always tell Tasha when I'm popping out to the shop, to let her know I won't be long. Joanne said Tasha has just managed to work out what the word 'shops' means, but to Tasha the association to that word was 'I'm not going to be in'. Tasha shared that she feels a little frustrated, because she would like to know what this word 'shops' actually means, as there are other times I leave the house but I haven't said 'shops,' so it confuses her.

Tasha offered an analogy – she said it's like someone sharing about their trip to the theatre and talking about how amazing the show was. She wouldn't be able to get involved with that conversation because she's never been to the theatre, so she'd probably just say, 'That's good,' and the conversation would be over. But if that person imagined Tasha was there with her at the theatre, and shared the experience with her using their imagination, then she could connect with what they were saying. She'd know what they were talking about and be able to share their enthusiasm and hold a conversation about it.

Tasha communicates by experiencing things, so she showed Joanne that when I go to the shops, she wants me to imagine picking her up and putting her in my bag, taking her in the car and talking to her as if she is physically with me as I'm driving. When I get there, I'm to take her in with me, and as I'm going around and buying things, I'm to tell her why I like certain things and share the whole experience with her. Then when I come home, I could ask her if she now understands what I mean when I say 'shops'. Tasha said she would love that, and that she's very curious about different things. She also shared that she's not physically brave enough to go outside, so experiencing these things in this way, using the Imagined Information Joanne has spoken about in her teachings, would give her an adventure.

Joanne said Tasha has an incredible imagination, and this allows her to experience things. Just because she doesn't do something physically, doesn't mean she can't experience it – she can, through me sharing it with her. She said I'm not really trying to do anything different when I'm chatting with her, as I'm still sharing the things I've experienced in my day. It's just so much work for her to try and work out what I mean, because she doesn't have any point of reference for the things I talk about, but she would love for me to share with her in this way so she can begin to understand what I'm talking about.

Curious to implement Tasha's request, the next time I went to the shop I used my imagination that she was going with me. I put her in the car, and I talked to her about things I could see on the way there. Then we got to the car park, and I shared that with her. When I got into the supermarket, I was so busy thinking about what I needed to buy that I'd forget to talk to her. I'd get part of the way round and suddenly think, 'Oh yeah, Tasha's with me,' and then I'd start telling her what I'm buying. I took her for a walk down the canal with me one day as well.

Since I've been sharing these experiences with her, we have gotten closer. She's not a cat who will sit on your lap and have a cuddle, but she does like to be with me and follows me wherever I go.

WHAT TASHA HAD TO SAY:

Mum cares so much about my well-being. She just wants me to be alright and will do anything to reassure me. She always keeps me informed about what's going on, and I want to clear up this matter about her talking to herself. It doesn't mean I'm not listening to her, it's just that sometimes I can hear her, but I'm not clear about the details so don't always answer her questions. She has been using her imagination and trusting that is part of our communication. She says it had even crossed her mind when she took me on outings in the car to put the seatbelt on me! She laughs, and wonders if people will think she is mad! I really appreciate her doing this for me.

Intention: TRUTH

Communication Exercise:

- Go for a walk, with or without your pet physically with you.
- Find a peaceful spot where you can stay awhile.
- Take a deep breath in, hold for a count of two, and as you breathe out, allow yourself to let go of tension from your mind and body.
- Do this a few times.
- Now lovingly call your pet to you and feel their presence as you imagine them sitting, facing you, their eyes looking deep into yours. (If you are with your pet, do this without calling them over to you physically. Use your imagination instead to connect with them.)
- As you feel the love emanating from your pet's eyes and know that they love you unconditionally, begin by sharing an experience or memory that still causes you a level of upset.
- Confide in your pet by sharing the emotions you're feeling and sensations you experience when you tell this story. Your pet is listening.

SENSORY SIGNS: EMOTION, SENSATION, KNOWING

Take a few moments to pause here and journal your experience.

CHAPTER 6

Compassion

Becky and her Male Dog, Brian

Dear Brian. I can still picture his face. Eagerly coming close, then backing off, then coming up close again. When Becky chose Brian for me to communicate with, I could immediately sense he had much to say, but it was stuck in his throat. Even his bark was hoarse. It made me connect with the experience of when you've had unexpressed words for so long, and one day someone gives you the opportunity to talk, or you've summoned the courage to speak out. What comes out is not loud and booming as you would have wanted, but hoarse, croaky, as if food has been swallowed and gone down the wrong way!

My heart just swells remembering how brave Brian was to speak out. He knew this was his chance. Becky had chosen him, out of her nineteen dogs, to be the one to communicate with me. I could sense how eager Brian was to put his request forward – he wanted Becky to write him letters.

WHAT BECKY HAD TO SAY:

I've spent a lot of years studying dog behaviour and helping people with their dogs' behavioural issues. It became increasingly obvious to me that the owner's view on why their dog does something can be entirely different to the dog's actual reasons, but I didn't know how to prove this. I wanted to learn to communicate with animals so I could ask the dog directly, so in 2012 I enrolled in a weekend-long workshop.

I have nineteen dogs sharing my home and my life! I refer to some of them as 'background dogs'. This is a term I use to describe the dogs who don't make too much of a fuss and tend to be overshadowed by the other dogs that require a lot of attention and care.

Brian was born in a kill shelter in Romania. From what I've been told, he wasn't taken out of the shelter by rescue workers until he was around six months old, meaning all he'd known until then was cruelty and fear.

Nine months old when he came to me, Brian was absolutely terrified. He hid away for weeks and had to have a children's sand pit as a litter tray indoors because he wouldn't venture outside. It took me nearly a year to be able to touch him, and even then, it was only while he cowered in a crate or hid behind the sofa.

He has now lived with me for six years, and although he's started to approach me for a fuss and a cuddle (usually when I'm sitting down), he still runs to his safe place when I stand up or if, without thinking, I reach down to touch him as I walk past.

Brian has needed a lot of work to build up his trust between us. It feels the same when I'm communicating with him. It's as if he wants to share things with me but is guarded and doesn't know how, or is too scared to. I've found my communications with him quite challenging because either I didn't get much of a response, or the information received would be what I'd already observed about him, which made me question whether it came from him. Although I can communicate with animals effortlessly, I still sometimes question the information that comes through from my own dogs because it may be what I already know about them.

Joanne was interested in exploring why I found it harder to communicate with my own dogs, and I was delighted I could nominate Brian for her to communicate with. Joanne explained she had checked that Brian wanted to have an open communication, and I was overjoyed with his reply. He just said, 'Why wouldn't I?' To know my nervous boy was willing to open up and have this extra connection with me was so heart-warming.

The session itself was fun and light-hearted, which helped me and Brian to relax. Joanne told me what Brian was communicating about wasn't like any request she'd received before! It wasn't something we could have guessed Brian or any other pet would ask for, but Joanne said since she now understood the extent of his nervousness, it made complete sense.

Finally, Brian was ready for Joanne to share with me what was on his mind – he wanted me to spend time writing letters to him! He asked for the letters to be put in an envelope and addressed to him. I had to put these in a post box that was just for him. He told Joanne once the letter was posted he would, at some point, reply to me. He said because we are connected, I would naturally receive a thought or would intuitively sense it was time for him to reply, and to be aware at this point to grab a pen and a piece of paper and start writing. What flowed through my pen would be his reply.

Joanne reminded me how our pets do bring something new into how they want their communication to be understood. Brian's request shows this is his communication style that he feels comfortable with, and he would like to experience this with me. It may not be how we think we would normally communicate with our pet, but Brian said he would like to try it for a period of one month to see if it helped us to communicate better with one another.

Joanne said communication can only happen if both parties are committed to it. Brian dearly wanted to have open communication with me, so I would make certain I heard his reply. Whenever I felt the need to say anything to him, I had to write him a letter, regardless of whether he'd replied to the previous one or not. When I put them in the post box, I was to release them and forget about them. This would give Brian time to process the communication and allow him to find the courage to open up to me and reply.

Joanne explained that our pets are just like humans, in that different personality types can have different communication styles. Some people don't like face-to-face discussions and prefer to send an email or talk on the phone, and some dogs prefer not to communicate telepathically with words but would rather send images or emotions instead.

She explained that by asking animals how they would prefer to communicate with us and putting their preferences into action, we'll experience easier-flowing communications. For example, in the past, if I wanted to know why Brian wouldn't let me stroke him when he is outside the crate, I would ask that exact question outright. For a dog as nervous as Brian, I could see how he might feel like I'm putting him on the spot and may want to shy away and not answer due to feeling pressured.

Writing a letter would be a softer and less direct way to approach Brian. I'm more heart-based when I write, and I find I'm able to be more objective when thinking about a situation.

With animal communication the answers may not be instantaneous, but I've learnt that once understanding has been reached resolutions do occur, given patience and time.

Through Joanne, Brian explained that because of the sensitivity of his energy frequency this was the best way to start to open up the communication channels with him and get to know him. The normal communication channels are too intense for him, and the example he gave did ring true for me. He said it's like if someone calls you or meets up with you face-to-face it can feel too confrontational, but if they send an email or write a letter you have time to absorb the information first and process it.

I came away from that communication session with a clear idea of how I was going to implement Brian's request. I had a shoe box I'd cover in wrapping paper and cut a hole in for the letters to be posted through. I would then cable tie it to the front of Brian's crate and use string to make the hinges for the lid to be able to close it down.

As I was making it, I suddenly became aware of hearing instructions in my mind. It was as if the information came from an outside source. I knew they weren't my own conscious thoughts, yet the words coming to me were clear. I turned around and Brian was sitting, looking up at me. Brian was directly communicating with me! This nervous boy of mine, who I'd struggled so long to hear, was now getting through to me loud and clear! He told me not to worry about the lid because it didn't need one. He wanted me to cable tie it to his crate with the back open so he could see his letters. It didn't need to be emptied – the letters were to be left in there.

He also said he wanted a plaque on the post box with his name on. I thought about typing his name and printing it out, but he said no. It had to look like a wooden plaque, with a paw print and a heart on it as well as his name – he was very specific!

I cut out another piece of cardboard, did exactly as he'd asked and stuck it to the front of the box, underneath the hole for the letters. I looked across at Brian, and he just said, 'See, we do communicate,' before turning around and getting into the crate. Oh, my heart filled with joy to experience this moment!

Keen to try writing him a letter, I did so straight away. As I wrote, he was replying almost instantaneously. I couldn't write his answers down without disrupting the flow of my letter, so I just continued. I basically had a telepathic communication with him as I wrote. I was over the moon that I'd heard his responses and that he felt he could answer everything, but I had also really wanted to experience what the act of writing to Brian would be like.

I have written more letters to Brian since Joanne's communication. Each time, the communication back from him was instant. He now communicates with me the same way the other dogs do as well. He'll walk up to me and look at me, and as I look down, he'll tell me something.

I've also started to make changes to situations indoors that he's brought up in our communications. I've seen a massive improvement in his confidence since doing this. He doesn't run to his crate so much anymore and will actually stand and be stroked. I've even had him come and lie on my foot as I've been standing doing things, which is something he'd never done before.

I can't believe something so simple has made such a big difference to our relationship. He has told me it's because he now knows he can trust me to do what he asks, and this makes him feel more confident. He now knows that if I do something he doesn't like he can ask me to stop, and I'll listen, so he doesn't need to run to a safe space anymore.

Joanne's communication with Brian has taught me so much as a communicator. It has shown me the importance of slowing down and allowing the communication channels to open.

Joanne is right – communication is a two-way thing. Talking and listening.

WHAT BRIAN HAD TO SAY:

I love these letters. They mean a lot to me, and I want to keep them. She doesn't really know what to do with them, but I want to keep them. The other dogs are starting to want letters as well, and I will allow them to be put in my post box.

I am so happy, because I now have a way to be able to hear what she's saying and know she's talking to just me. I also have the chance to understand what she's saying and respond accordingly. She even bought me a Christmas card. Thank you!

Intention: COMPASSION

Communication Exercise:

- Connect with your pet using your imagination, pausing a while to sense their presence.
- Close your eyes.
- In your mind, reach out to your pet and gently stroke their body. Offer this loving touch, knowing your pet will receive this as a communication from you. Spend as long as it is comfortable for both of you to enjoy this experience.
- As you stroke your pet, let them know how much you care about them.
- With each gentle stroke, send them the feelings of reassurance, calm, understanding and tenderness.
- Trust that your pet will receive this communication from you.

SENSORY SIGNS: VISUAL, EMOTION, SENSATION

Take a few moments to pause here and journal your experience.

CHAPTER 7

Togetherness

Cheri and her Female Turtle, Gamera

Gamera was a long-standing member of Cheri's family. Since Gamera was a pet Cheri couldn't cuddle, or even have on her lap, she wondered if this meant they were missing out on their bonding time. Cheri didn't know if she needed to spend time just sitting next to Gamera's tank with her, and she also wasn't sure how to get the conversation flowing as she found Gamera was usually 'quiet' with her words. Gamera was thrilled to share her views on what types of conversations held meaning and which were not so important. She added that it's not about being physically together that defines connection, but what occurs emotionally and spiritually.

WHAT CHERI HAD TO SAY:

I've been able to communicate with animals since childhood and have always felt a deep connection with them. I trust them immensely and feel closer to them than I do humans. I'm the sort of person who steps over ants in the street, and I rescue spiders in my house and release them outside. I love all animals, bugs, and nature, but I never realised I was communicating with them. I just thought I could read their body language. I knew animals so well and so deeply that I just seemed to know what they wanted, but I never saw it as me communicating telepathically with them.

I live in Japan, and an animal communicator would occasionally be featured on a television programme about animals. As a family, we always looked forward to the episodes she appeared on and thought it amazing she could communicate with animals like that. I decided to see if she offered private sessions, as I wanted to get her to connect with my own animals. I then attended one of her courses, including learning about chakras and reading auras.

Then I started reading and researching, just absorbing as much information as I could. I started taking animal communication training courses from a variety of communicators to hone my own skills.

I realised everyone has the ability to communicate with animals. It's not something we have to learn, but rather something we have to remember how to do.

After doing quite a number of courses, I finally found my way to Joanne, and she supported me in gaining the confidence I needed to put my knowledge into action. Joanne is full of ideas and utilises a variety of ways to encourage and support those of us in her Community Group to help us gain confidence.

I didn't doubt that Gamera and I had a connection, or that we were communicating well when it came to knowing when she was getting hungry or how to meet her physical needs, but I yearned to have a deeper understanding of what she enjoyed about her life, and how she experienced the relationship with her human family. Mostly she was quiet in nature, and interacting with her was quite different compared to how I'd interacted with my dogs in the past.

I really wanted to develop a more meaningful relationship with her. My concern was that I didn't want her to just sit in a tank in the corner of the room and be lonely.

When Joanne connected with Gamera, she told Joanne she usually likes her communications to have a purpose to them. She said she likes the word 'projects'. She likes to have something that takes you from A to B, then to C, and has continuity, so doesn't want to have the types of conversations that are 'on and off', or where they are just dipped in and out of. She said the example I gave of interacting with a dog or a cat is the type that is ongoing without a purpose – when they're on my lap or in my face, they just want their needs met at that moment. In contrast, Gamera is looking for a long-term communication and the commitment from me to share that with her.

Gamera said it wasn't improvement we needed, but rather finding a communication style that would work for both of us. She didn't want me to sit with her for a certain length of time and meditate with her, as she did that enough on her own and didn't need me to do it with her. She wanted to have a purpose to our conversations – some important project she and I could plan together, and suggested it be a year-long project so as not to be rushed. She said doing this would help to get the conversation flowing, because we would have a shared purpose to the conversation.

Joanne said Gamera had a fluid way of sending the information to her, that it felt like she was immersed in water and was very gentle. She could feel when it was something Gamera was getting excited about or that was important to her, because she'd feel ripples and waves getting stronger through this water.

Gamera was inviting me to swim with her as a way of relaxing myself before communicating with her. I knew Gamera meant this as an imagination exercise. I could swim with Gamera as I meditated to connect with her. Gamera suggested ways to ask her a question and then wait to see how she shared information through the imagery and sensation of water and how it felt. Was it calm? What was the temperature like? Was it bubbly? Were there crashing waves? These are the ways she can communicate with me when I ask her yes or no questions, questions around how she's feeling, or around what's happening at the times when she's shedding her shell.

Without giving any details to Joanne about what type of year-long project Gamera wanted, she simply told Joanne that was for me to work out. While Joanne was relaying this to me, I suddenly received an image in my mind of a book with all of our conversations written. I could even see the title *Wisdom from My Turtle: My Chats with Gamera* on the book cover! I knew there and then that was a direct communication from Gamera to me. I loved the idea of the book being a year-long project, suiting the pace Gamera said she wanted to go at. It would be a conduit for her to be visible to the world, through me.

I've never written a book, but having received this information so clearly, I knew it was what she wanted me to do. Gamera wished for her teachings to be shared out into the wider world, and she couldn't do it alone. She needed my help, and said this would make spending time with her exciting. Finding something in common we could both work towards and quietly exchanging ideas would allow the communication lines to open between us.

Gamera is very wise, and I feel her wisdom all the time. Although we've just started our year-long journey together writing the book, we've been enjoying time spent together in meditation. While using my imagination to swim side-by-side in the water with Gamera, I see her on my right-hand side as we swim together through the ocean. We're so connected there's no need for words. She tells me to relax and enjoy the experience of swimming with her through the beautiful water.

She's very patient and doesn't mind taking things at a slower pace, and I think that's another reason why we're doing a lot of swimming together at the moment. She's not pushing me to ask her too many questions, happy to take the time to build up the connection between us first. She's such a wise, loving soul, and a great teacher. I look forward to sharing her teachings with the world.

WHAT GAMERA HAD TO SAY:

I feel so alive with this book idea. Every day I wake up and wonder what we're going to talk about for it, and there's no impatience. It's just the fact that I know we have this ongoing project I can tap into every day. It makes waking up and staying up a pleasure, because I can move my energy through this idea.

I'm able to initiate more conversations now, and when Cheri thinks about the fact that she hasn't written something, that's me popping into her thoughts. It's not to nag her. I'm just happy I can initiate that and ask her if we can do some writing on that day. When she suddenly thinks about a book cover idea or a book title, that's me sharing my idea with her and initiating a conversation with her.

Intention: TOGETHERNESS

Communication Exercise:

- Find a time when you and your pet are feeling relaxed and you'd like to offer one another undivided attention.
- Think of an activity you both enjoy doing.
- Describe this activity to your pet by using your imagination.
- Recall the time when you both participated in this activity and imagine your pet being able to access the information from your imagination.
- Be clear and colourful with your description, including sound effects, smell, taste, emotions – sensations you can conjure up so the experience is as real as you can make it.
- Trust that the more vivid and clear your imagination is, the more your pet can access the information from your mind.
- After a few moments, you can stop sending the information to your pet.
- Now it's your turn to receive any image, sound, smell, taste, emotion or sensation. All you have to do is to be in 'receiver mode'. Go with the flow and be open to what comes through to you. Allow your pet's imagination to send you the information your pet wants you to receive.

SENSORY SIGNS: VISUAL, SOUND, SMELL, TASTE, EMOTION, SENSATION

Take a few moments to pause here and journal your experience.

CHAPTER 8

Communication is a Loving Act
Understanding Both Perspectives

I used to wonder if I was 'doing it right' when wanting to communicate with my pets. I wasn't sure whether I should say it out loud to them or close my eyes and meditate in order to be in a trance-like state so I could project my thoughts to them. It felt both confusing and silly sometimes, yet at the same time, I also knew that however I did it, somehow it would work.

I think back to times I've fleetingly thought about my cat, wondering where he was when it was close to his dinner time. Lo and behold, a few minutes later he'd appear at the door, asking to come in. Another example would be when I'm expecting a visitor, but I've kept the routine the same and made the effort not to show any emotion, yet my dogs would be restless and over-sensitive to any noises or my movement until the time the visitor arrived!

There's no doubt our pets can sense our emotions, but they wouldn't know our exact thoughts. When we give our pets verbal instructions, it is often accompanied by body language such as pointing, looking directly at them, or physically guiding them to where we want to move towards, hence we intervene to ensure they respond accordingly.

When we choose to communicate with them without the use of verbal or body language, instead using the 7 Sensory (intuitive) Signs, we can offer a much more detailed explanation for what we wish to convey to them.

I often need to explain things in more detail to Mhyah than to my other pets. Mhyah is a very cooperative dog and often does as I ask, but this doesn't mean she understands the reasons behind my instructions. She can feel slightly confused or frustrated when she doesn't see my point of view. For example, when I'm out walking with her there's a bridge we cross to get to some woodland. Along the bridge is signage to say dogs are required to be on a lead. I call her to me and put her on the lead, and she'll ask why this is necessary, telling me she is reliable with her recall and in her assessment, there are no dangers. I explain that humans have rules to follow, even if at that moment it doesn't appear to be relevant. The funny thing is, because I'm explaining it to Mhyah, I really do see her point of view. Looking around, there's not a soul about, and I too wonder why I'm obeying the rules in that present moment!

Communication is a loving act.
The key for communicating with our pets is understanding both perspectives.

As mentioned before, the more we focus on learning to converse in their language, the easier it is for us to understand their perspective, and vice versa.

Now we come to the next three stories of a cat, a Labrador and a Husky who ask their owners to communicate with them in most subtle, yet compelling ways.

CHAPTER 9

Understanding

Emilie and her Male Cat, Kiki

Kiki. A dear boy. Quiet in more ways than one when indoors, yet a confident explorer outdoors – two sides to one story. Emilie's relationship with Kiki was centred around his indoor character, so she saw him as homely, timid and a reluctant mama's boy. For Kiki, he had two worlds that allowed two expressions of his whole personality. When he was off out, he was Kiki the adventurer, staying out for days at a time and connecting with the sights, sounds and smells along his travels, often without the thought of missing home or his mother. Emilie, on the other hand, holding on to the indoor perspective of Kiki, would worry about his safety and ability to fend for himself when outdoors. With my guidance, Emilie has had numerous communications to help her understand Kiki more, and has worked to improve her ability to connect with Kiki as a whole. This has given Kiki freedom and he now knows his connection with his mother is one of autonomy.

WHAT EMILIE HAD TO SAY:

I've been working on my animal communication with Joanne for around two years now. She's been essential in helping me to understand my cats. Over a period of time, I have taken care of the stray cats near where I live, and a number of them chose to live in my home. I felt relieved they were now safe and had a roof over their heads and food to eat, but in terms of forming a relationship with them, I felt completely lost. I was aware stray cats needed to be handled differently to domestic cats, but I needed Joanne to help me to facilitate the communications with each of them so we could come to a harmonious arrangement for sharing the indoor space together.

My biggest battle with animal communication is managing my own emotions, as often they get in the way of receiving clear information. Being sensitive to energy, I practise meditation using breathwork to ground myself so as not to get overwhelmed. Sometimes it's not easy for me to do this on my own. I know I need to stop myself from overthinking things so communication can flow.

I love all my cats, but there is something special about Kiki. He came to live with me around two and a half years ago. I care so much about his wellness. I always wonder if everything is OK with him – if he's eating enough, or if he's happy. When he's outdoors, I often tune in and ask him what he's doing, or where he is. The way I would experience Kiki connecting back with me was a warm sensation entering the energy centre of my heart chakra, which is situated around my chest area. For a while now, I haven't felt this when I ask Kiki to communicate with me. Even if I did receive an answer to my question, I began to doubt whether he was replying, or if it were my own thoughts coming into my mind.

I admit that most of the time I need to communicate with Kiki is when he's outdoors and I haven't seen him for some time.

My worry creeps in, wondering if he's safe and when he'll return. I was desperate to feel that connection again, just to be sure his replies were true. I strongly wanted to be able to have a deep conversation with him, instead of feeling like I was catching bits of a conversation here and there. As my doubt grew, I started to believe Kiki was the most difficult of my cats to communicate with, so I knew I wanted Joanne to connect with Kiki to help me with this struggle.

As I relayed all this to Joanne, she checked in with Kiki to find out if there was a reason our communication had not been as forthcoming as it used to be.

Kiki started the conversation by telling Joanne he respects me for not bombarding him with questions all the time, and he's very grateful for that. You see, in the past, when he wasn't home, I'd ask him lots of questions. 'Where are you? What are you doing? When will you be home? Why aren't you home yet?' This was the result of my over-worrying and needing to know he was safe. This was brought up in a previous communication with Kiki, so I'd made a note not to intrude on his time when he was out enjoying himself.

Kiki confirmed that now when I ask to connect with him, I am respectfully checking in with him. I'm also being honest with him by sharing that I do worry when he stays out longer than he usually does, and also that I miss him and feel lonely without him at home with me. Kiki said this acknowledgement has helped us both to understand one another better.

Having initially entered the communication session with Joanne thinking my connection with Kiki had lessened, it was wonderful to receive confirmation from Kiki that he appreciates the way I am approaching him. In fact, he told Joanne I had already worked out the best way to communicate with him, so Joanne didn't need to tell me how else to improve on it!

Joanne shared that Kiki provided an analogy. He said to liken our communication channel to a cat flap – sometimes it's open and swings both ways, sometimes it just swings one way, and sometimes it's completely closed. When the cat flap is open and swinging back and forth the heart chakra energy is balanced and Kiki can connect with me, heart-to-heart. When I ask him a question he can reply easily and I know without doubt it is him, but when it's closed he can't do this. This made me smile. I know whenever I look at the cat flap from here on, I'll remember what Kiki said!

Kiki then asked how open my heart chakra was for those times when I couldn't experience the sensation in my chest area when I requested a connection with him. This was a useful question and made me realise that often events in my life, or a situation that may have occurred during the day, can affect my emotions and cause my heart chakra to close down. I knew then I needed to do some internal work to open it back up when that happens. One way I could do this was to practise expanding my toroidal field.

Joanne then suggested I also work on Kiki's toroidal field. This wasn't something I'd thought of doing before, but when she explained that all matter has a toroidal field, and hence animals too, it made perfect sense that I could also expand Kiki's toroidal field. I just had to replicate the process I use for my own, visualising the energy flowing upwards from the direction of Kiki's heart, up through his head, out, then down the sides of him and up through his paws and back to his heart. Then do the same again, and also visualise the energy flowing from his front and back and upwards through his head, down his legs and up through his paws, back to his heart. I was aiming for us both to be in a place of receiving great energy.

Joanne commented that I'm proof to other communicators that when we really listen to our animals it makes it easier for them to converse with us. They usually want to, it's just that if our channels aren't open they can't accept our communication

– and can't get through to us either. So it wasn't that Kiki was difficult to communicate with, but that I was struggling to trust the information Kiki was sending because I was swamped by my own emotions.

Now I've started to open up my heart chakra again, I'm listening to Kiki more and connecting with his emotions, rather than being overwhelmed by my own, and the communication has improved. He now sends me emotions, sensations and imagery, and I trust the communication I have with him.

I've learned to listen to Kiki and understand how he wants to be approached for communication – without pressure – and not to bombard him with my doubts. He's also learned the best way to communicate back to me, knowing that by sending me reassurances that he is safe, I can relax and accept that he's having a good time being outdoors. It was wonderful to hear from Joanne that Kiki came through in the communication session to share that he appreciates the style of communication I'm already using. What a boost to my confidence!

WHAT KIKI HAD TO SAY:

Emilie's communication was fine, and her method was right, she just needed to continue to open up her heart chakra so the information could come in more consistently, deeper and more quickly.

She's really working at that. Her love for me allows her to do it, but I'm not asking her to rush it. I don't want her to rush it. It's already happening, but the opening of a heart chakra can't happen all at once when there have been situations that have made it more protective.

I feel like I've been able to help with the healing of the heart chakra, and that's what I want to do. Communication-wise it's really good – we both communicate beautifully, so I want her to embrace that and receive it. I'm proud of her.

Intention: UNDERSTANDING

Communication Exercise:

- Does your pet have a habit or a certain behaviour you don't understand?
- How about a habit or a certain behaviour you have that your pet doesn't understand?
- Connect with your pet by calling them to you using your imagination. Experience how they show themselves to you. Do you see them, or do you feel them?
- Share with your pet a habit you have. Using words, pictures, sound, emotion, sensation, smell and taste (where applicable), using your imagination, explain to them why you have this habit.
- Now it's your pet's turn to share with you their reasons for having a habit that you are curious about. Allow your imagination to come into play. Keep an open mind for pictures, sound, smell, taste, emotion and sensation to be received as your pet's communication to you.

SENSORY SIGNS: VISUAL, SOUND, SMELL, TASTE, EMOTION, SENSATION

Take a few moments to pause here and journal your experience

CHAPTER 10

Curiosity

Tracey and her Female Dog, Sandy

Seeing the Invisible. Let's make it into a game. That's Sandy's wish – to have Tracey create a game they both would enjoy, then communication becomes part of this game. Sandy doesn't view communication to be only for those times when humans announce, 'Let's talk.' Often, we communicate more when we share an activity. That activity engages our ability to interact, negotiate, exchange opinions, and thus create an environment of letting the day-to-day distractions be put aside. Guessing games would be a favourite for Sandy and Tracey!

WHAT TRACEY HAD TO SAY:

Sandy came to me a few years ago. I aimed to train her to be my assistance dog. I have a few health issues, and was looking to retire Jack, my senior dog, and have Sandy replace him for the work.

Sandy was difficult to train. She kept pulling the lead out of my hand and not following my instructions. My animal communication journey started when I contacted a professional animal communicator to help me understand what was going on with Sandy. It came through that Sandy didn't want to be an assistance dog. As soon as I found out I stopped her training and decided she could be just my pet dog. I love her so much and didn't want to do anything against her will.

After some time had passed, I wanted to have another communication, however the animal communicator who originally communicated with Sandy had stopped offering her services. Then I found Joanne on social media. I wanted Joanne to have a communication, initially with Jack, and then a further session with Sandy, to check how they were both feeling and find out how they felt about the role they played in my life. Joanne could confirm that Jack was a true natural when it came to supporting me as an assistance dog and loved his work.

With Sandy, I learnt something new. Sandy said that although she didn't want to be an assistance dog, helping me with the practical day-to-day tasks, she still saw her role as supporting me and described herself as a spiritual assistance dog. I loved this idea, especially knowing both my dogs wanted to help me.

Sandy also communicated that I could explore energy healing so we could share this in common, so over the next two years I signed up to various healing courses and enjoyed learning and practising on myself, friends and family. I then progressed to studying animal communication with Joanne, joined her **Community** Group, and have been a member ever since.

When Joanne suggested communicating to ask how our own pets want to communicate with their parents, I just knew I wanted to do it with Sandy. I find I'll do the odd communication here and there, but because they're my dogs and I know them, I never know what to talk to them about. This means I only ever really connect with them when there's something wrong, so it's never fun to communicate, for them or me. I would dearly love to have a flowing conversation with Sandy, almost like how I imagine it would be talking to another human being.

During the communication session, Joanne asked Sandy if she would like to have the same style of communication that I wanted – general day-to-day chit chat that we can just switch in and out of. Sandy replied that she did, but those communications with me were usually about things that one or the other of us didn't really want to talk about. She mentioned the dreaded phrase 'we need to talk' and said I tend to set aside a specific amount of time to talk about issues, often of a serious nature. I tend to have something to eat, grab a cup of tea, then I sit down and say, 'Right, now we can talk.'

Joanne explained that wasn't the sort of everyday conversation Sandy wanted. Sandy said she wanted to be able to come into my thoughts at any time of the day and tell me about something she's just heard, seen or smelt. Sandy reminded me about how responsive she is when I give her verbal instructions, such as 'go into the garden' or 'go to bed'. Sandy does it almost instantly. Sandy would like the conversations to be more from the mind, likening it to Joanne's Imagined Information that Joanne had shared to describe how she experiences communications with animals.

Sandy suggested playing 'brain games'. She really wanted to try out some games to increase the fun aspect. Her first suggestion was like a kind of guessing game, but taking the guessing out of it by using **Imagined Information**. One of the games could be when I let her out into the garden, for me to stay indoors. Sandy would then use the sensory (intuitive) signs of visual, sound, smell, taste, emotion and physical sensation to tell me when she was ready to come back in – without me going to have a look outside to check on her first. I was to allow Sandy to enter my thoughts so she could communicate with me, and to use that information to act upon her requests accordingly.

Sandy also suggested another game involving her KONG® toy. Joanne suggested I fill the KONG® with goat's milk yoghurt and freeze it so it's like an ice lolly, then give it to Sandy. She said Sandy can then enter my thoughts to tell me when she's finished, and I can go and take a look. Sandy wanted me to start trying these things and wanted to practise popping into my thoughts in this way. She said this would be a great way of practising my animal communication skills while having fun with her.

Now the conversation was centred around games, I too began to experience the communication flowing with Sandy, which I hadn't before. And to prove this is a topic of interest to her, Sandy continued by showing Joanne an activity she'd like to do that involved me making a toy for her. She said she didn't want me to go out and buy any mental stimulation toys. I could save money and make them.

This particular activity involved me getting a large cardboard box and filling it with upright toilet roll inserts. I then had to put treats inside some of the toilet rolls and not others so she could find them and work out how to get them. She said this was an activity I could give her to do in the evening when she was pawing at the carpet and not settling.

This was not what I had expected, but I'm so glad she could tell me the topics of conversation that would be good for us to share. Often, I don't think about checking in with my pets to ask what they want to talk about. This made me realise that, in the past, I'd only communicated with Sandy when something was wrong, so it makes sense that the conversations then would be more difficult.

Sandy used the analogy that I was always the one who made the initial phone call, but now I can also allow her to get in touch first. I used to think I had to be the one to open up the communication channels in order to speak to my dogs, but Sandy showed me she can come into my thoughts and share things with me whenever she wants to. Maybe she'd been doing this already, I just hadn't realised and wasn't aware she was talking to me.

Since the session with Joanne, I've been putting some of these suggestions in place. I play the guessing game at different times, but I haven't made the box game she mentioned yet. We did buy her a moving ball for Christmas, and she loved it. I haven't seen her play like that for years.

WHAT SANDY HAD TO SAY:

Mum is working on what she knows and sticking to the bits from the challenge that she's been getting to grips with. I'm really enjoying it. I love these games.

I've been a bit naughty though and have made it slightly difficult for her, so it's not that Mum isn't getting it. I just do things sometimes and then change my mind. When she tries telepathically to guess what I'm doing she doesn't always get it right because I change it, so she shouldn't think she's wrong.

There's something else I'd like her to start doing any time I'm not in the room, but I also don't want her to feel like she has to do it all the time. I'd like her to hold something that belongs to me when I'm not there, such as when I'm on a walk or something, and I want her to focus on this object and use it to really connect with me. It would be a form of psychometry. She could even give me something that isn't dog related, like a crystal or something, so it's just mine, then use this object to connect with me in this way.

Intention: CURIOSITY

Communication Exercise:

- Close your eyes and sniff the air. I mean really sniff the air.
- Let your awareness bring to you the smells, aromas, fragrances – both subtle and strong – that are around you now. Be curious. Can you identify what they are?
- Think about a dog's nose – the structure and function of a dog's nose. Imagine what having a dog's nose would be like if you could experience it from their perspective. It's known that dogs can smell separately with each nostril.
- Now connect with your pet by calling them in your mind to come to you. You can do this without being with them. Visualise them coming to sit in front of you.
- Gently touch your pet's nose with your nose. Ask your pet to share with you what they like to smell with each nostril. Imagine your dog is sniffing the ground on a walk in the woods, or the air when they're at the beach.
- Start with the left nostril. Take your time.
- When you're ready, ask your pet to share with you what they like to smell with the right nostril. Be very present in that moment.
- What images, emotions and tastes are conjured up when you detect the various smells, aromas and fragrances?

SENSORY SIGNS: SMELL, TASTE, VISUAL, EMOTION

Take a few moments to pause here and journal your experience

_____

_____

_____

_____

_____

_____

_____

_____

_____

_____

_____

_____

_____

_____

_____

_____

_____

_____

_____

_____

_____

_____

_____

_____

CHAPTER 11

Healing

Jason and his Female Dog, Skyla

Skyla brought with her some known and unknown aspects of her past history when she came to live with Jason and his family. Often, as pet parents, we wonder whether the issues our pets present result from negative past experiences, but let's also consider for a moment that having faced many challenges, our pets also possess power, strength, resilience and courage within themselves. They show us that no matter how traumatic their lives have been, they can find it within themselves to overcome adversity. Skyla brings to Jason her ability to connect with energetic information, where one does not rely solely on needing physical proof. Instead, energetic information is far more powerful and revealing.

WHAT JASON HAD TO SAY:

I first got into animal communication around fifteen years ago. I came across it on the Internet and remember thinking, 'I'm not sure if I believe this is possible, but if it is, it could have a profound impact on the world.' That's what motivated me to learn more about it.

I found a workshop in the next village. It was just a one-day workshop, but I came away having experienced myself being able to relay a lot of accurate information when connecting with the animals. It was an incredible experience knowing the potential to help animals and people with this. From there, I purchased study material and attended several workshops to further my learning, then progressed to completing an Animal Communication Professional Practice course. I set up a website, and since then have been offering professional communication consultations alongside animal Reiki.

I came across Joanne several years ago when I joined her Community Group. We'd collaborate together, whereby if one of us didn't have immediate availability for client bookings, the other would step in to help.

Skyla came to be in my family two and a half years ago. I don't feel like I get anywhere when I communicate with her or offer her Reiki. She'll sit with me while I stroke her, but when I start a Reiki session, even at a distance, she gets up and moves away within a few seconds.

I know animals sometimes do this and can still receive the healing from further away, but I just wondered why she wouldn't settle beside me, as we have quite a close bond. I believe she understands what I'm saying to her, but I just don't seem to get anything back in terms of answers or knowing how she feels about what I've said. Although Huskies are normally known to be active, Skyla is very chilled out and reserved. There is definitely something special about her, but I've never been able to pinpoint what that is. When Joanne shared her idea for exploring together with our pets what could help improve communications, I knew I wanted to involve Skyla.

Joanne began the communication session by checking with Skyla that she understood that the reason was to find out how to open up a conversation between the two of us. In my mind, I had two specific topics I wanted to bring to the session and hoped Skyla and I could speak to each other in a way that would make it easy for her to interpret and respond to.

The first was to do with the clipping of a claw. Normally, Skyla would be fine with this activity, but there was one claw that had been causing a problem and she wouldn't let me cut it. I didn't understand why she would let me do the others, and not this one. I wasn't sure if what I was saying to reassure her was helping or not, as we couldn't get past this one claw.

Skyla confirmed to Joanne that I have good communication skills and she feels we are quite open with each other, but when it comes to her physical body, she feels quite protective towards that.

Skyla showed Joanne the visual of a surgeon laying out their surgical kit, with everything marked out. She said that if a surgeon was going to operate, everything would be set out in a certain way, and everyone would know what was going on. So even though she's been fine with the claw clipping before, she would like me to approach her in a similar fashion.

Skyla doesn't just want me to visualise the process of me cutting her claws while telling her she's safe, I'll be calm with her, and it will be over and done with quickly – she needs me to convey everything to her through my visualisations from the moment I pick up the clippers. She wants to know what they are, how I hold them and how I'll hold her paw – basically every little detail about the process.

I have to think of her as a child who asks a million and one questions about what we're doing, and give the answers using the sensory sign of visuals. Skyla explained this is because she is genuinely interested in knowing what I'm doing every step of the way.

Joanne said Skyla was sending such lovely emotions about the communications. She was saying she needs to be understood and needs this level of detail, then she'll show me how much of a difference it makes.

The second thing I wanted to discuss with Skyla was the fact that she had started to leak urine occasionally. Mostly on her bed, but sometimes on the carpet. We'd seen the vet, but it was inconclusive as to what was causing this issue. Joanne asked Skyla how best I could open up the conversation around such a sensitive topic with her, and if Skyla knew how to resolve this health issue.

Skyla responded by suggesting I could check her bladder or reproductive system energetically. She said I could refer to an anatomical chart, and energetically scan the areas of her body systems. This would ensure she could communicate by guiding me to specific areas that needed healing.

Interestingly, this is something I've experienced when working with clients' pets in the past and for case studies. I have been able to connect with the energy of the areas where the pet is hurting, or which part of their body holds an energy imbalance. It's always been quite an accurate practice, yet I hadn't linked it to doing this with Skyla. As a Reiki practitioner, I could offer this to Skyla.

Skyla said she'll guide me with the sensory signs of the physical sensations she feels in each of the areas as we work through them. This could be heat, sensitivity, pressure or weakness. She said she wanted me to be open to working with her in this way and that it would take a bit of practice, but I would eventually get to know what feels right and wrong or balanced and unbalanced. Once I've established this, she says, I'll be able to use this technique for any part of her body.

She shared that this will be huge moving forward, because her physical health is important to both of us. This will give me the sense that I can be of use to her in this capacity. She said she knows I get frustrated and I see it as her 'shutting down' when I don't feel I'm getting anything back from her, but she says it's just because she's hypersensitive to physical sensations as well as energetic sensations. For example, I may just be stroking her gently, but for her the feeling is very intense, and it's the same with energy healing.

Understanding how hypersensitive Skyla is has helped me come to terms with her moving away when I offer her Reiki. It must be too intense for her to accept it at the distance I offer it. I'm going to try a visualisation with her for this, one where I show her a dial and ask her to use it to turn the Reiki energy down to a level she finds acceptable.

Joanne explained that we don't often make communication easy for our animals. They have to do a lot of the understanding and interpretation, and we make them work for it! If we can make it easier for them, then the conversation will open up and flow. This is particularly important if we want to ask about a sensitive subject. When it comes to our own animals, it's usually only sensitive subjects we want to discuss, usually to do with a health complaint or a behavioural situation.

Joanne was right – the two things I wanted to discuss with Skyla fell into those categories. She said our pets want us to see things from *their perspective*, and when we have that understanding we'll enter a different relationship.

This was all making perfect sense to me. I felt empowered to try these things and take my communication with Skyla in a different direction that would be more comfortable for her.

Moving forward, I printed off all of the anatomy diagrams and I'm looking forward to finding out what physical sensations she's going to send me. Joanne joked that I'll be getting a real physiology lesson with her! Little did she know I've wanted to look into canine anatomy for a while but never gotten around to it, so this has been a reminder to action something that interests me.

Skyla

WHAT SKYLA HAD TO SAY:

Yes, I am supersonic sensitive and everything is magnified. As soon as Joanne said 'Hello' my ears were exploding. I need everything turned down a bit and things need to be done a lot quieter. That's why I'm so visual – it's like a silent film and a lot easier for me to handle.

If I loved my dad before, then I love him even more now he's doing this for me. He is such an amazing dad, not just to me but to his human children as well. I do view him as a dad, but I also view him as a friend. The friendship is growing more as he communicates with me. I don't want friendship to take over the parent role though – I like being one of his kids!

I feel like he could be my soul mate if we can open up the

communication channels. I'd like that, but I don't want him to put pressure on himself. He doesn't need to think about how to do this. I'm loving the process and the journey I'm on with him. What he's doing really resonates with me and I'm finding I'm a lot more receptive to things because of him.

I don't want him to confuse my physical capacity with my spiritual capacity. With the communication he can help me to move towards the true essence of who I am. If he continues to work with the visualisation and does the medical intuitive work, then he'll eventually help my physical body to meet my essence. That's my path to learn, but he can play a big part in helping me with it.

Intention: HEALING

Communication Exercise:

- Choose a time when you are both having a rest or when it's bedtime.
- Close your eyes and bring your awareness to how your body feels. Starting from the tips of your toes, move up slowly along each part until you reach the top of your head.
- Take note of one area of your body you would like to receive healing for.
- Bring your pet to mind and ask their permission to receive healing from them. Allow yourself to open up to accept their healing.
- Share with your pet why this part of your body needs healing. Allow yourself to confide in your pet, knowing your pet is listening to you.
- Continue to rest as your pet sends healing to this part of your body. Drift off to sleep if it is comfortable for you to do so, and when you awaken, thank your pet for their healing.

SENSORY SIGNS: VISUAL, EMOTION, SENSATION, KNOWING

Take a few moments to pause here and journal your experience.

CHAPTER 12

Listening and Talking
Over-questioning is not Communication!

Do you chat to your pet about everything? Do you get home from work and start telling your dog all that has happened to you? How about your dog? I bet she too would love to share with you about her day. Perhaps she's been out walking with the dog walker, or she's been home all day but has news to tell you about what she could hear through the walls and saw looking out the window. Your dog would love you to listen to her too!

I used to struggle with knowing what topics to communicate with my pets about, what questions to ask them. Often, it's only those times when my dog is stressed or not doing as I ask that I think about communicating. I can do that verbally, so I wanted to use animal communication as a way of holding longer and more meaningful conversations, but it seemed as if I'd only get a word here and there, rather than being able to converse as I would with people.

At one point, I thought communicating with my pets was about me finding out what they need, how to fix them, and how to help them. In time, I learned that they too needed to know how they could help me, and what restrictions I have to face living in the world and the society I'm in, and how that could affect them. Then it became such a beautiful experience to share from both perspectives.

Let's look at what communication is not – it is not just about questions and answers, that is, us asking them questions all the time. I used to say to my dog Donny, 'Why do you do this? Why do you do that? How come you're doing this again? Can you not do this? Can you just be like that?' So he said to me, 'You are pestering me.'

Over-questioning is not communication!

I fall into this trap often with Donny because he has lots of chronic health issues – and there's nothing worse than a pet parent who is worried sick and not finding ways to resolve the issues. I used to repeatedly ask Donny questions such as, 'Why don't you tell me what's going on? If only you told me what's wrong, I could get it fixed.'

We need to remember that communication is a two-way conversation. Just as with humans, listening is as important as talking. Think of the times when someone either asked you questions you didn't feel comfortable replying to, or when they just talked *at* you, and you began to feel as if your opinions didn't matter. Good communication allows both parties to share in an open and easy manner, imparting a sense of togetherness and understanding. This is similar when you communicate with your pets. Listening and talking.

When our pet displays behaviours we don't understand, it's up to us to find out how our pet wants to converse with us. What if our pets are the ones who have questions for us? This didn't cross my mind at first, as often I would assume they know everything. It's true they can sense our emotions and the energy of the words we speak, but they certainly don't know the details or specifics of what is going on. Imagine how that must feel. To sense that something is in the air but not know what or why, hence the only way to react accordingly is to respond to what they perceive, rather than the actuality. That's why when we say to our pets, 'Hey, everything is ok, don't worry,' they still can overreact.

Our pets appreciate receiving details that can help them to respond better to the situation we put them in. Now let me introduce the concept that your pet can also give you details and specifics when it comes to situations they need help with. The next three stories of a dog, a cat and a horse demonstrate this, each in their individual way.

CHAPTER 13

Hope

Piedad and her Male Dog, Platón

Platón. What a story for how this dog came into Piedad's life! Can it be that an animal can manifest their desired home with a human? We know of the Laws of Attraction for turning dreams into reality. Could Piedad's specific wishes have linked in with Platón's true needs energetically, and somehow these met in that one moment which then created the reality?

Piedad worried that her household of chitty-chatty kitties was drowning out Platón's voice, so she chose to work with Platón to find out his suggestions for improving their conversations. It turned out Platón has a passion, and when Piedad learnt more about how Platón feels and connected with this passion, it became their shared topic of conversation. During the day, Platón is happy to merge into the background of the kitties' social interactions, but when nightfall arrives, it's Platón's turn to have his time with Piedad.

WHAT PIEDAD HAD TO SAY:

I actually got into animal communication by chance. I belonged to a group concerned with how animals in the wild conveyed messages to us, and the lady who ran the group shared a story about Joanne. A bit later, she shared about a workshop Joanne was teaching about communicating with animals. That was the first time I heard about animal communication.

I've always liked animals and lived with them by my side, so I knew this was something I would love to do. I needed to see if this was actually possible. I signed up for the workshop and absolutely loved it, deciding this was something I wanted to integrate into my life.

Joanne has been my only teacher. I read a bit about animal communication, but that was after I'd been working with her, so she has taught me everything I know.

When I started, I only received enough information to fill two or three lines of writing. Joanne always told me it was beautiful and came from my heart, which made me feel like I was doing well and had to keep going. Joanne also taught me to trust the information I was receiving, and this has never left me. I've gone through every situation and challenge in my animal communication journey with trust and confidence, and I have to thank her for that.

Two years ago, I told Joanne I was thinking about adopting a dog from a shelter and I was worried about how our four cats would take it. She suggested using what I'd learned and asking them what kind of dog they would like. I loved the idea and communicated with my cats about it. Two of them, Ondina and Tabatha, told me they wanted a calm, quiet, adult dog. I could even visualise the face of a dog in the conversations with them. Nunilo told me it would take her some time to get used to the dog, and Figaro said that as long as the dog left him alone, it was OK with him.

I searched for a dog on the website of a shelter near my place, and there he was! A three-year-old dog who looked like the dog I'd visualised in my communications, and according to the description, he was the calmest, sweetest, most kind-hearted creature. His name was Nuko, but we thought Platón suited him better. He came home a few days later, and I was so pleased to see that he and the cats were fine together. It proved to me that the communication I had with my cats was real.

I wanted Joanne to communicate with Platón, because my conversations with him always seemed non-existent. I would talk to him, but he didn't seem to answer me and there was no flowing conversation. I knew he listened and heard me, because he was showing me he understood with his physical actions.

Platón's eyes give a lot away, and I can usually tell from his behaviour and his body language what he needs. If he wants to go out, he just goes to the door. If there's no water in his bowl, he looks at me in a certain way and I know exactly what he needs. However, I notice I normally communicate with him when there is something wrong with him, or when I want to give him a choice. For example, if we're on a walk I'll ask him which way he wants to go. He'll make the decision and head in the direction he wants. So, he listens and gets the information, but I don't get anything back from him other than his physical response. I would love to have a conversation in my mind with him and hear his answers.

The first thing Joanne did was establish that Platón was clear with the intention of what she was doing in this session, and he shared his approval with her. She said she was receiving a visual of him slowly nodding his head in approval. He then shared with her the feeling of excitement in the upper abdomen area (energy centre for solar plexus), but again it was subtle. He told her he does do exchanges of conversation, but his delivery is quite slow compared to me, as I speak quickly. She told me to imagine the type of mood that would be evoked if classical music was playing in the background.

I resonated with the nodding, because I do sometimes see the slow nod when I'm talking to him. He shared that quite often I would start a conversation with him, but because of the pace he converses at, I usually get distracted and start doing other things just as he's starting to talk. He said either this or the phone might ring, or the cats come and take over and have a fleeting conversation with me, then go again. He shared that what is actually happening is that he's getting interrupted, and because of his communication style, it's easy for the extroverted animals to come in with their busier energy and draw my attention.

Platón then told Joanne he would like to hold conversations with a shared interest and would like it if I was interested enough to learn about that. Joanne then asked if we have an interest we have in common. I had to really think about it, because Platón is quite a lazy dog during the day and doesn't want to go out for walks or do anything. He's more of a night-time dog.

He seems enthusiastic when I put my boots on to go for a walk, but we walk about ten steps and he turns to go back home. He's half Wolfhound and half Spanish Mastiff, he has the hound part that really loves sniffing. He finds night-time walks very interesting because of the wildlife outside and wants to go out almost every hour to check what's going on and what animals are about. He loves to be out there, sniffing out all the activity. I go with him, so this is something we already do together that we could expand on. I do sometimes lose him in the dark, but when I call him, he comes straight back. I appreciate that, because although I want him to enjoy himself, I also want him to be safe. He already knows that when night-time comes it's our time, and he pulls me out of the house. So it's something we already share, and that I think is special for him.

I need to get more into that hobby or activity of scenting and tracking so the spontaneity between Platón and myself will be there, where he'll then offer me conversations based on tracking and scenting. He says this will happen during the day as well, not just at night-time, because he knows I want him to initiate these conversations with me. He admitted he knows that sometimes I wonder if he thinks he's being ignored or left out because I haven't spoken to him, and it's always me asking him things and trying to check in with him. He's happy for me to continue to work in this way, but it doesn't ignite him, and we'll just be carrying on as we are. But as we're talking about this shared activity and the wild animals his energy is waking up. This exercise would be about the two of us sharing a common interest, and the more I learn and become fascinated by all the animals that are out there at night, the more the communication channels will open between us.

It seems as if we do just expect our own animals to know what we're thinking, and we take it for granted they'll pick up on these thoughts. Platón confirmed they do get it, but he said that knowing what I'm thinking doesn't mean he knows I want him to be involved. I probably have hundreds of thoughts a day that he knows about, but I don't necessarily want his input, so how does he know which ones I want to discuss with him and which ones I don't?

Currently, when it comes to the walks, it's like we're both enjoying the same things separately as we're not involving each other. He went on to explain that for me to experience what he loves, during the day or at night, gives us content we can use in conversation and the spontaneity will happen throughout the day. He said just because he's not moving in the day doesn't mean he's not planning, and he'd love to include me in his plans. Once we get used to sharing things like this, he'll start to accept that it's ok to intrude into my thoughts and will start to share other things with me. He also said we can do this without physically doing anything, because we can discuss things and plan what to do when we go outside, or I can research tracking online and share with him the things I'm reading and finding out.

Everything Platón suggested sounded great to me and I've been implementing it all. I don't do it consciously, but I know he now knows I'm aware of how much he loves this activity. I share his interest in following the tracks. We find the wild boar faeces, or the holes the badgers make, or the hoof prints from the roe deer – I so enjoy sharing those things with him.

The night is so special, and everything is so different compared to daylight. Sometimes we get carried away by everything and I feel so bonded to him. The bond between us has become stronger since we've been sharing these walks in this way.

I've also come to learn that he doesn't talk much because he's not a talker. He shows me his emotions and uses the look in his eyes to tell me how he's feeling and what he needs. He's not a man of long conversations and I respect that. I may have longer conversations with the cats and other animals, but now I know this is how he is and it's not just him not responding, I don't mind.

Animal communication isn't about changing the animal to suit us. It's about letting them have a voice and allowing them to be heard.

We tend to have a lot of expectations when it comes to communicating with our animals. We need to forget those, because it's only really about getting to know each other and having respect for each other, especially with an older dog like Platón. He was three years old when he came to me from the rescue centre, so he already had issues and his own personality. I respect Platón, and he knows this and appreciates the respect I have for him. I think this has also contributed to making our bond stronger.

I didn't expect what came up in the session. I thought it was going to be different, and that Joanne was just going to give me some hints about how to approach him. I suppose she did, just not in the way I was expecting. If we try to get something from our animals and we're not getting it, then of course it's time to try something different, instead of just repeating the same thing and hoping for a different outcome.

Although this approach was different, it definitely helped our relationship and communications. Now I'm even more conscious, in the sense that I'm not just watching him enjoy himself, but I'm sharing his enjoyment and other emotions. He's also much happier since I've been doing this. When we come back home, he comes in and runs in circles and spins around. I just know he's happy and grateful.

WHAT PLATÓN HAD TO SAY:

I understand that we haven't been able to go tracking together, but I'm tracking even when I'm not outside so I can save up stories for her. I can save up these experiences, smells, sounds and tastes so she doesn't have to go with me. I can do it myself and share it with her, so I'm going to be initiating a lot of conversations. I'm enjoying it and would love to go hiking on a trail or a track where you go somewhere unknown and have adventures. I like to save up experiences and stories to share rather than having a daily chat.

Intention: HOPE

Communication Exercise:
- On a piece of paper, draw two circles side-by-side.
- In the middle of one of the circles, write the name of your pet.
- In the middle of the other circle, write your name.
- As you focus on the circles, ask your pet to join you by requesting for their presence to be felt near you. Close your eyes if you prefer, and use your imagination to ask your pet to help you feel them near you as if they are physically next to you.
- Share with your pet a wish you have for them. What would you wish for your pet? Write it down in the circle that has your pet's name.
- Then ask your pet the question, 'What would you wish for me?' Be open to receive the answer as an image, thought or word. The first image, thought or word that comes to you, write that down in the circle with your name in it.
- Hold the paper in your hand, close your eyes and gently blow on the paper as if you are blowing the wishes into the air.
- Feel the emotions and sensations that rise up for you.
- Open your eyes when you feel ready.
- You can choose to keep the piece of paper or release it with love.

SENSORY SIGNS: VISUAL, EMOTION, SENSATION, WORD, THOUGHT

Take a few moments to pause here and journal your experience.

_____

_____

_____

_____

_____

_____

_____

_____

_____

_____

_____

_____

_____

_____

_____

_____

_____

_____

_____

_____

_____

_____

_____

CHAPTER 14

Power

Judith and her Female Cat, Zoe

Poor Zoe. Sickly Zoe. Traumatised Zoe. This was the physical and emotional relationship Judith shared with Zoe. Understandably so, as Judith was the assigned foster carer of this very unwell cat. It was almost endless and tiring, with vomiting, diarrhoea, poor appetite and withdrawal behaviours at the forefront, yet Judith held faith, 'There is more to Zoe than meets the eye.'

I was reminded in an instant that no matter their weakness on the physical level, never to forget animals have a spirit, and that spirit is always infinitely more powerful than their body.

Zoe was adamant she didn't want the focus of conversation to be about her physical needs. I felt her strength, her fierceness, the need for her voice to be respected and her instructions adhered to. I would have questioned that strength had I met her in person, but because I connected via photo and therefore first and foremost energetically with her, Zoe could bypass her physical body and bring my attention to her spirit. Her true essence. She did not want pity. She did not want tears.

WHAT JUDITH HAD TO SAY:

I learnt of animal communication around eighteen months ago, when I first saw a video about it online. Straight away, I believed in it and could see how it could be possible. I bought a book that completely opened up the idea that it is of course 'a thing', but it's so deep – it's only the first step of a person's animal communication journey. I like to truly understand things, to grow my soul and to be of service, so I threw myself into learning more about this wonderful phenomenon.

Ask most people how their pet came into their life and they've got this lovely story about how they went to the breeder or rescue and just knew they were the pet for them. It was completely different for me and Zoe. I'd moved into my new house and just had this need to be of service. I had previous experience volunteering at shelters, so headed to the local rescue and offered to foster a cat. I remember walking in and saying, 'I want to help a cat that has been abandoned, alone, and has the saddest story please.' And out came Zoe.

Zoe was an unusual cat. She didn't like to be handled and was known to bite. I regularly tried to communicate with her. Originally, I just sat with her at a time when she was quiet, comfortable and relaxed and would talk to her out loud for a bit, then try to connect from my heart to ask how she was. I would sit and pour love into her, welcome her to my home and tell her she was safe, but I rarely seemed to get anything back from her. Most of the time, there was this overwhelming sense of a door closing shut, as if she was telling me she just didn't want to talk.

Zoe then became so unwell that most of my attempted communications turned into me trying to find out if she was OK, asking how she was feeling, what was wrong with her and what I could do to help her. I was becoming increasingly frustrated at not being able to connect. I longed to be able to find out what Zoe needed, or if there was something else I could do to meet her needs.

I am a member of Joanne's Community Group, which was where I heard that Joanne was looking for communicators who were struggling to communicate with their own pets. I knew that would be an amazing chance for me to learn how to enhance my animal communication skills to communicate with Zoe.

Joanne initially checked in with Zoe to see if she wanted to have the same type of communication with me that I'd mentioned I wanted. A more open, back and forth, ongoing type of conversation. Joanne explained to Zoe that my particular concern would be about her physical and emotional needs, particularly after she'd just spent a week at the vet clinic as an inpatient due to the vomiting issue that caused me great concern about her health.

I was taken by surprise, as the first thing Zoe told Joanne was that she wanted to discuss whether or not I viewed her as weak, fragile and vulnerable. She knew it would have been coming from a pure heart and a place of wanting to care for her, but it was important for her to know whether this was my overall opinion of her.

It had never occurred to me, but I realised it was very possible that I did. Her story and background were quite extreme and tragic, so may have cemented a 'poor Zoe, the victim' mentality that preceded everything else.

Joanne understood this. She said when we rescue a pet it's a human trait to tell everyone they're a rescue. Something within us taps into their story, but we have to be mindful of the energy we're pouring into it. Constantly labelling them as a victim of their past won't help them to move forward and grow. She made it clear it wasn't that their past wasn't relevant – they'll still carry scars from it – but they don't necessarily want it at the forefront of everything they do from now on.

She said Zoe would love for me to see her as strong in her divinity. Her energy wasn't able to expand and she wasn't able to come out of her shell because she was being judged by her physical body. I had to start recognising how strong she was to have survived the things she had and to be where she is in her life now. I had to remember that her physical body was just one aspect of her. Just because she had gone through trauma, that didn't mean her spirit wasn't strong. In fact, her spirit would be stronger because of the physical trauma.

She said it wasn't about not acknowledging her past, but about seeing her as more than just a victim of what her physical body had endured. She missed communicating 'spirit to spirit' and said if I could connect with how amazing her spirit is and how bright her light is, then she would love to communicate with me. Zoe replied that it was purely a mindset. The moment I recognised her as a powerful being, it would change everything.

She said it would be challenging, because there would be times when she would be looking very frail, but I would still need to look past that. It's hard for a human to do that, to see a pet unwell and continue to recognise their magnificence. But if I could do it, then she would open up more to me and the conversation would flow every day. All I had to do was recognise that just because she was ill or had suffered physical trauma didn't mean she'd lost who she was. She could still love, breathe and live. She still had desires and interests.

I had to start afresh with her, a clean slate, and speak to her about things that would help her to enjoy talking to me so she would look forward to our conversations as something that would brighten her day and help her to open up to me. Joanne told me to embrace the fact that her physicality is a concern and that I had to watch her, but to remember to check in with her other aspects each day as well. She said to think of mind, body and spirit. She said if I've checked in with her body, I then need to ask her about her mind and spirit as well.

Joanne said this is what all communicators should be aiming for with their own pets. We should be moving past the formalised questioning. We need to be encouraging a natural conversation to flow continuously.

She said to think of it like talking to a friend. We might chat at various times of the day or send constant messages, but if we had a falling out, we'd make time to sit and talk it over.

We always expect that when we ask our pet a question we'll receive an instant reply, but sometimes they may not respond for a couple of days, and sometimes they don't know the answers.

By not sitting there formally interviewing them, we can ask the question and release it, and they can answer in their own time. Just as with people, conversing with our pets is a two-way activity.

At first, I didn't know whether I could actually do that, so Joanne offered the analogy of visiting someone in hospital. She said they don't just want to talk about how ill they are. They'll ask us about things we've done and want us to share about the food we've had if we've been out for a meal, or the film we watched if we've been to the cinema. She wanted me to help her tap into the pleasures of life and the wonders of higher consciousness; that was what conversation was all about to her. I could resonate with this information, because although my concerns for Zoe's unwell state tended to overwhelm me, I could also see she was strong and feisty, like no cat I'd ever known before.

Joanne checked whether Zoe had any advice on the best way to do it. Zoe said just to listen, connect with her spirit, and shift my way of viewing her. This wasn't about fixing all of her physical problems. It was about getting me to see what was beyond those. Even when the physical problems weren't there, I was wasting time and energy looking for answers as to what they were and why they'd gone. She wanted to take my focus away from this so I could get to know *all of her* better.

I understood all that Zoe had brought up in her communication. The one thing I can do is to see her as a whole – mind, body and spirit – and this would shift the relationship.

Not long after this session with Joanne, I found out I was no longer required to foster Zoe as the shelter had a potential home for her. What I learnt from Zoe I now use to help my other foster cat, Peanut.

WHAT ZOE HAD TO SAY:

There are still challenges with my health, but I know Judith is trying, looking to rise above the day-to-day tangible things she's having to help me with on a physical level. The challenge is there, because to rise above and connect with the spirituality and higher self of an animal when the physical body is going through challenges isn't an easy thing to do. I chose Judith so that both of us can connect with that higher energy.

The higher energy is what will see her through. She'll get caught up with the physical stuff, but if she doesn't connect with the higher energy, she'll be consumed by the physicality of the challenge, so she needs to keep with it. She is doing it, and I understand it's a lot to ask from her, but I really need it. I need her to remind me of my higher energy, because then I can hold onto it.

Intention: POWER

Communication Exercise:

- Have your pet physically with you.
- Create a quiet and relaxed space to spend some time together.
- When you and your pet are feeling settled, ask your pet whether they are comfortable for you to place your hands gently on them. Proceed if they show you that they are.
- Keep your hands in the same place on your pet for a little while and bring your attention to how your hands feel.
- Close your eyes if you wish.
- Are you aware of any tingling, buzzing, warmth, coolness or spontaneous movements of your hands?
- Now move your hands so they are an inch or two away from your pet's body, still around the same area you had physically placed your hands beforehand.
- Again, keep your hands in the same place for a little while and bring your attention to how your hands feel.
- Are you aware of any tingling, buzzing, warmth, coolness or spontaneous movements of your hands?
- Ask your pet to share their energetic power with you. Imagine them switching on their energetic field power from the mains plug.
- Allow your pet to send you sensations in your own body, such as vibrations, tingling, warmth, coolness or spontaneous movements as they connect you with their energetic field.
- When you feel ready to stop, ask your pet to 'disconnect' you from their energetic field power. You can do this by imagining them switching off from the mains plug, allowing you both to release the connection.
- Open your eyes and relax your hands back to your sides.

SENSORY SIGNS: VISUAL, EMOTION, SENSATION, KNOWING

Take a few moments to pause here and journal your experience.

CHAPTER 15

Connection

Verena and her Female Horse, Ronda

Dear Ronda, whose sensitivity and ethereal-like interaction with Verena displayed itself as if she were emotionally and physically distant at times. Ronda is happier conversing as a 'collective consciousness' about intergalactic and ultra-dimensional subject matters, while Verena's concern for her darling horse was about her physical health.

I had to persuade Ronda to 'stay' in her physical body and consciously converse about this. Often, animals don't hold the same priority as humans do with regard to their physicality. Ronda almost sees it as a waste of time, the way humans obsess over what is wrong and the efforts to fix our physical health.

WHAT VERENA HAD TO SAY:

I was inspired to learn more about animal communication because I've been interested in metaphysical and spiritual subjects since I was a little girl, so began by reading a few books and attended a course in 2011. There were so many different people there. Some were new to animal communication and others were already pretty experienced.

Initially, I found it difficult as I felt so blocked. I think it was because I was approaching it in terms of being right or wrong and compared myself with others, who in my opinion, were getting all of these amazing communications while I wasn't. For example, those people could get all of this information from the animals, such as where they lived and the colour of their food bowl. It was information I believed I should be receiving, but I just wasn't. I thought I couldn't do it. As much as I was being told that everybody has the ability, I just thought I was the exception.

I had Ronda at the time. She's always been a big motivator for me to learn more about animal communication so I could understand and communicate with her. I also wanted to open myself up so she could understand me.

I continued to look on the Internet and found Joanne on a specialist learning website offering support as part of her Community Group. I immediately clicked with her teaching style and loved it.

I put Ronda and myself forward when I heard about Joanne wanting to explore why communicators generally felt they found it difficult to communicate with their own pets. I fit into this category, because I doubt myself all the time when I want to communicate with Ronda. An example would be keeping Ronda's hooves clean. Sometimes she would let me, other times she wouldn't, and I easily got frustrated about it. Over time, I developed a way of communicating with Ronda about this. Now I just have to point at her hoof and she'll lift it for me. This proves that our communication is much better around this subject now.

Yet I still struggle in other areas, especially when we're out on walks. It's an important aspect to keep her healthy with this form of exercise; however, in her mind, when we're out it's just about eating the grass! I try to compromise with her and tell her she can eat at the end. Occasionally this works, but more often than not she has a different idea to me and just wants to stop and eat. That's one part where I feel our communication is breaking down, and again, I get quite frustrated. The other is when I'm trying to find out what's going on for her health, because I still doubt the information I receive. I'd love to improve our communication so she cooperates more and lets me know when there's something I need to take care of physically.

When first connecting with Ronda, Joanne was quite taken aback at Ronda's directness. Joanne was trying to find a nicer way of relaying it to me, but eventually she just came out and said it. 'Ronda is questioning you about how much you really know about taking care of horses.'

I was startled by this question from Ronda. It wasn't what I expected at all! As far as I was concerned, I knew quite a bit about horse care and didn't understand why she would even be asking that.

Joanne then asked whether I had expanded on what I already knew on the subject and grown my knowledge and learning. I had previously looked into a number of complementary and alternative techniques around the subjects we were discussing, wanting Ronda to be treated as an individual and have her own personalised regime of care, but have not invested in the time needed to put it in action yet.

Joanne explained that Ronda was expressing that at the present time there was a gap in what she needed and what I was offering her. She needed her treatments to be individualised, and therefore wanted me to continue my search and expand my knowledge. Ronda was sure there was still more I could learn, and that I could find someone who understands what I'm looking for and will work with me to achieve that.

Joanne then explained that when we communicate with our pets, they normally draw on the knowledge we already hold. If what I had was mainly from the mainstream approach, and she was seeking complementary or alternative ways, then the communication couldn't develop further when I'm asking Ronda what she needs and how I can help her. This made me determined to continue my search and believe there had to be someone out there who could help us.

Although it was a bit hard for me to hear what Ronda was saying to me, I understood deep down what she meant. Joanne said that in actual fact, my own frustration around these issues is that I know I still haven't found the right person to help Ronda, and I know that the things I'm doing at present don't feel right and aren't aligned with me.

During the session, I was aware I could feel a shift happening within me. Before this communication I'd almost lost all hope of Ronda getting better physically, because she faces numerous health challenges. Now I felt a renewed sense that my searching might not be in vain and there might actually be someone who knows how to help Ronda. When I reflected on Ronda's initial question, I could resonate with it in a different way. I realised she wasn't insinuating that I didn't know anything about caring for horses, but that I must continue to search for what else there is to learn and find that I haven't yet explored.

There was a time when Ronda's health deteriorated and she wasn't able to get up off the ground. This spurred me into super-quick action, and by speaking to several people and asking for advice, I found a couple who were energy practitioners, recommended by a neighbour. I'm so grateful I did, because with their help Ronda's condition began to improve both physically and emotionally.

Since the communication Joanne facilitated, my own communication with Ronda has gone from strength to strength. Over the last few weeks, I've been able to feel that her energy levels are more stable and she appreciates being able to enjoy her life. I'm aware now I may not have all the answers to help Ronda, but the more I learn and grow in my knowledge, skills and understanding, those experiences will certainly benefit Ronda, giving her greater input into how I continue to take care of her.

WHAT RONDA HAD TO SAY:

The energy between us is so much lighter and there's a lot more laughter. It has helped me not to feel like I can't make a mistake. It's almost like there's no such thing as perfection, standards, goals or tasks. It just feels much more playful.

I feel she is able to connect more with my emotional needs and also my physical needs. I now feel like I can lean into her. I am letting my guard down more and I don't feel like I need to wait until she has the perfect solution.

Intention: CONNECTION

Communication Exercise:

- Close your eyes and imagine yourself standing at the end of a bridge.
- Your pet is standing on the other side of this bridge.
- The bridge is a symbol of the connection you share.
- As you take the first step onto the bridge, be aware of how this bridge appears to you.
- Take another step.
- Keep moving forward until you reach the midpoint of the bridge.
- Now it's your pet's turn.
- As your pet steps onto the bridge and moves towards you, let your pet share with you how the bridge appears to them.
- When your pet reaches the midpoint, you can both take your time and fully experience the connection you share.

SENSORY SIGNS: VISUAL, SOUND, EMOTION, SENSATION, THOUGHT, WORD, SYMBOLISM

Take a few moments to pause here and journal your experience.

CHAPTER 16

Good Conversations
Harmoniously Resolving Issues

I remember when, with Donny, I'd only think about using animal communication to find out what was wrong, wanting to fix whatever was going on for him. Donny is the dog who would have itchy skin, or be reactive when he saw other dogs, or he'd be scratching his ear or licking his paw. I found myself only communicating questions that began with 'why'. 'Why do you do this? Why can't you stop? Why can't you tell me what you need? Why are you barking so loudly when the dog that walked past you did nothing?' And so it went!

I never received an answer from Donny! In the end, I'd conclude that either he didn't want to communicate with me, or I was doing it wrong so it wasn't working.

In time, I learnt that Donny wasn't interested in communicating only on the topic of 'what's wrong'. I started to be more aware of how I approached him, and to understand that he would much prefer to share conversations about things he finds enjoyment and pleasure in. So I would make a point of having shorter and more frequent communications with him, communicating about our walks (he loves being outside), about food (definitely his favourite subject!) and about his animal companions. Donny appreciates being listened to when he talks about his relationships with Mitch, Ziggi and Mhyah.

The beauty of communicating with your own pets is it's something you can do daily, and you can do it three or four times in a day. It can be something you don't do for about a week, and yet you can pick up where you left off. And to me, that's what it's really about – they are with us, we share a life together, so communication can happen any time, informally as well as formally.

A great advantage of being able to communicate with your pets is to help with harmoniously resolving behavioural challenges. It's best that you converse about their specific behaviour outside of the situation. You may think, for example, when your pets are overreacting at that moment, that's when you want to say to them, 'What's going on? Tell me.' And if they told you, you'd be able to help them. However, I assure you this can be overwhelming for your pets, trying to express themselves while they're dealing with a stressful situation.

For example, I was communicating with Ziggi when he came home looking distressed, and he went to hide under the bed. This was out of character, and I immediately felt panicked, wondering if he was hurt. I kept asking him what was wrong, asking him to come out from hiding so I could physically examine him, but no amount of communication could coax Ziggi to converse with me or approach me. In the end, I realised that was not what he needed. Instead, I turned my attention to slowing down my breathing and relaxing my body. I stayed quiet, while sending him the message that he could take his time, and when he was ready, to come to me.

Once again, this is similar to how it would be for you if something frightened you or made you really angry, and somebody repeatedly asks you, 'What's the matter?' or says, 'You need to calm down.' You wouldn't be able to truly connect with what it is you're feeling or experiencing in that moment because you're just reacting.

The important part is you have to keep an open mind and heart, because it's their perspective you're receiving. When you become too fixated on resolving an issue, it's likely you'll lose sight of the fact that your pet will be answering from their perspective, which may not be what you expect.

What if you and your pet don't agree on a particular subject? How does this hinder coming to a joint agreement and resolution? Communication doesn't mean your pet has to do what you say, just because you've explained it to them.

The key is establishing an understanding whereby both parties have the opportunity to share their side of the story.

Next, in the last set of three stories, a cat and two dogs show that when their human companions listen to them, and I mean *really listen* to them, their behaviour can naturally shift to reflect how important it is to be heard.

CHAPTER 17

Empowerment

Debbie and her Male Cat, Tiger

Tiger. Independent. Self-knowing. Street smart. Tiger's role in Debbie's life was to provide consistent support, companionship and an anchor. All the upheaval of life-changing events that led to Debbie and Tiger sharing a life on their own, together, meant Tiger had an important role to play in Debbie's life. Debbie regarded physical security as the top priority in her role as pet parent to Tiger, but this clashed with Tiger's perspective. What Tiger classically did was offer a 'No comment' response to her communications around this discussion, leading Debbie to believe communicating with Tiger was not easy. However, this was a tactical move on Tiger's part!

The lesson here is to know that in order to entice our pets into a conversation, we must first ensure our agenda matches with theirs!

WHAT DEBBIE HAD TO SAY:

My first experience with animal communicators came in May 2018, when I attended my first Animal Energy World Conference. I was familiar with several of the speakers through my energy work with humans, and was already qualified in personal training, sports massage, reflexology, Emotional Freedom Technique™ and aromatherapy.

I'd spent several years taking care of other people's animals too, and became eager to incorporate all my holistic therapies to bring pets and humans together for mutual healing. Deciding animal communication could help me do this, I attended various courses and continued to expand my knowledge to work with animals, which included using the Emotional Freedom Technique™, animal healing, sound healing and Akashic records to heal animals and people at a soul level.

I approached Joanne to help me hone my animal communication skills, and it was during this time that Joanne announced her idea to work with communicators who were finding it more difficult to communicate with their own pets than other people's pets.

I wanted to participate with Tiger, whom I'd been with for six years. He was my late father-in-law's cat. When my father-in-law died, Tiger didn't have anywhere to go so I just took him in, moving him to our home in Wiltshire. He soon became my cat. We moved later that year to Devon, then I got divorced and moved to another place in Devon, and now I've moved to Cornwall – so Tiger has had five homes in the past six years.

Originally a rescue cat, Tiger had only been with my father-in-law for three years. Before that, he'd been moved between two or three foster homes, so I always felt very guilty about having to move and uproot him.

Our marital home was perfect to start with because Tiger had a field behind and had his own little patch. In time, he started going down to the corner of the main road, then across it, to sit in the hedge and look for mice. I'd be so worried each time I saw him head over that way, as I knew it was risky with the traffic.

Then I moved to a derelict pig farm, giving Tiger a lot of space to roam around in. It was so perfect for him that I almost bought the house I was living in. Unfortunately, there were plans for a lot of building work in the area, meaning his access to all the farmland would be restricted. I then thought people might move into the finished conversions, and may own dogs, meaning Tiger might roam even further to find a safe place. This was one of the reasons for my move to Cornwall, where I bought a new house that backed onto fields. I thought it absolutely perfect, but after I moved in, I discovered that another 150 houses would be built on the field behind!

Tiger loves to hunt and catch mice, it's his favourite thing to do, but the building work going on at the back of my home does restrict him. He still goes out, but he's a bit hesitant in the day, because he's listening all the time to the work that's going on. I look forward to the weekends, as the building work stops and I know Tiger can have free access to what's left of the field. I wanted to find out how this situation was actually impacting him. I kept feeling I was letting him down and failing in keeping him safe.

I have a lot of fears around the building work and what it will mean for Tiger. I want him to be able to be himself and to be happy, and because he loves to be outside, I want him to have a safe outside area to be in. Tiger is the focus of my life – I moved houses to accommodate him, and would happily move again if it's what he wants.

Joanne connected with Tiger to see how he thought we could get our communications to a place where we could discuss these things freely. He agreed we were missing conversation. He said my sensory signs for visuals were strong, but they were painting a really dark picture that blocked the conversation between us. He said he would love to have a discussion with me where we chatter back and forth, talking about how his day has been. He knew I wanted this too and he would love to tell me that.

Joanne explained that Tiger's sensory sign for visuals is extremely sensitive. What this means is whatever I visually send to him, he receives it ten times stronger, compared to a less sensitive being, and I should bear in mind how this would impact him if the information I sent him was all about danger warnings. Tiger explained that instead of focusing on the dangers, he preferred to have strategies. He likes facts, information and planning, showing Joanne that it's like having a meeting with an agenda and minutes.

Tiger then told Joanne he'd like me to view him as smart and streetwise. He reminded me that he used to live in London, so was familiar with traffic. I explained that I haven't forgotten, but I personally feel it's very different as there was continuous steady traffic in London, whereas here it's so unpredictable.

Joanne suggested the conversation reflected the fact that he's smart and streetwise, and I had to connect with that and not view him as naive or unaware. As I paused to do this, I suddenly remembered the times I'd observed him listening for the machinery from the building site, and how he'd stay close if he heard it. Then he'd work out the times the workmen had their tea breaks and lunch breaks and would shoot over there, find a mouse while it was quiet, then come back home! Joanne said he was reminding me what he could do, and he said I needed to trust him.

Tiger's attitude was that if you're worried about something you have to put a plan together, rather than just going over the worst-case scenario and worrying. And he made it clear how much it would mean to him if he could share his stories, and for me to marvel at his amazing adventures. He'll be able to send me visuals, and I'll be able to get an insight into his life outside and what goes on for him on a day-to-day basis. He also wanted to show me that he doesn't do anything foolish.

Tiger told Joanne that when he does things I'm telling him not to, I have to respect his need for freedom as he wants to retain his adventurous spirit. He doesn't want this whole situation to turn him into a house cat, because he would hate that. Joanne checked how to go ahead with this. Tiger said it was purely about me allowing him to tell me what he's doing, without asking any specific questions or sharing any dangers with him – I have to be in listening mode. So, when he shares something with me that I am aware is a possible danger, I have to hold onto that information. When he's finished, I can give him the plan or strategy for that. I don't need to point out the dangers in his story, because he already knows them. This would be a new way of conversing with him.

We decided to try it there and then, during the session, to see what Tiger wanted to share with me. I connected with him and got an image of him out on the hedge going along the fence. He shared where he found a mouse nest and said, 'Look, this is a good area. If I stay here for a while, then I can just pounce on them.' The communication was so clear.

Then he told me he wasn't so worried about what was going on in the field or the building site, but was more worried about this other cat who kept trying to steal his water out of his watering can. It was a big, black fluffy cat he'd had a fight with a few days previously. He showed me an area on the hedge where he can keep the cat out, so he had that covered, and said the cat isn't around so much during the day, it mostly turns up at night-time.

Joanne told me to continue to converse with him in this way and let him present information to me, and from this I can get an idea of what his priority dangers are. He was now showing me the sort of things he needed my help with. He'd already started working out a plan to avoid the cat, but he obviously needed me to help with it. He was bringing forward something that to him was a higher priority, danger-wise, than all the other things I'd been worrying about. That's the beauty of animal communication – we can see things from their perspective.

Tiger said this is the exact way he'll converse with me about other issues as well, including his health, behaviour, food, etc. He said he sees me as the person to go to with his problems to help him work things out, but it's hard for him to bring things to me if my attention is fixed on something else, because he can't get in to tell me about other things that are bothering him.

Gradually, after the session, and taking on board all that Tiger communicated about, I have managed to stop worrying. I'm no longer constantly looking out the window when he goes out. I'm a lot more relaxed. Tiger's communication made me realise that a lot of the issues around his safety were because of my own fears I was projecting onto him. All I needed to do was accept that he could work it out himself, and that he knew I was here and he always had a safe home to come back to.

It's bizarre how, as communicators, we can find it so challenging to communicate with our own animals! I've realised that unless there was something wrong, I never sat down and had a proper conversation with Tiger. I always assumed that because we were in each other's presence all the time, we would know what was going on in each other's minds. Hopefully, we can now enjoy more spontaneous communications and share topics of interest.

WHAT TIGER HAD TO SAY:

It means the world to me that Mum trusts me, but I also want to add a little disclaimer. Just because she trusts me doesn't always mean she is going to stop worrying about me, and I understand that. I don't want her to feel bad about worrying.

The fact that she reminds herself that she trusts me makes me feel like my opinion counts. I'm not being dismissed – she sees me as bigger than I am and respects me. She understands that in the outside world I can probably cope better than most humans, because I know the ins and outs of what's going on and I'm smart. I'm quick, I can work things through, and she remembers this. It won't always be words when we communicate. It will be an emotional and physical experience too. It's about her hearing me and allowing me to help her overcome her fears. I'm very proud that she trusts me.

Intention: EMPOWERMENT

Communication Exercise:

- Offer your pet choices so you can make decisions together. Next time you're at the pet store, use your imagination to call your pet to join you.
- As you browse through the food, toys, books, etc., share the specific items by sending images, sensations and words to your pet.
- Alternatively, when shopping online, invite your pet to choose an item or two they would like!
- With situations that require bigger decisions, such as a house move or whether to have a new pet as an addition to the family, spend time communicating the scenario of your plans. Allow your pet to share their feelings and views about the changes ahead.

SENSORY SIGNS: VISUAL, SOUND, SMELL, TASTE, EMOTION, SENSATION, THOUGHT

Take a few moments to pause here and journal your experience.

CHAPTER 18

Humour

Tanja and her Female Dog, Maja

A duo team. Often, we view our responsibility towards our pets with such gravity, placing great pressure on ourselves to care for them to the highest standard. To prevent illness and injury, to stop all their stresses and fears, and to only provide a safe haven of well-being becomes a tall order.

In many ways, Maja has had enough seriousness from her previous home. Tanja too, as her dog Niela had many health issues and has since passed away. Tanja's relationships were clouded with grave concern before Maja joined the family, so now is the time to start afresh for Tanja and Maja, using humour as their communication bond.

When Tanja and Maja's relationship shifted from pet parent and pet to become more like sisters, a closer connection happened!

WHAT TANJA HAD TO SAY:

I started looking into learning animal communication in 2008 because I very much wanted to communicate with my own dog Niela (now in spirit). I thought it would be great to know what she was thinking, to have conversations with her, to help her and to have fun with her.

I initially went on a basic course with a teacher who brought animal communication to Germany. During the course I got good results when practising with other people's pets, and my interest started to grow. Unfortunately, the tutor had also mentioned that it's generally easier to talk to others' pets, but not always easy to communicate with your own. I took this on board and discovered I did indeed find it difficult to communicate with my own dogs.

I continued learning, completing several other courses to advance in my animal communication study, and I joined some online groups. Thereafter, my practice was sporadic. I'd communicate with other people's pets in person and online, but didn't have the momentum to keep going.

Then Niela passed away. I desperately wanted to have a connection with her, so I started looking into animal communication again. I read books and searched online, until I found Joanne through a website where she hosted a practice group.

Everything changed for me! I suddenly became part of a community and could speak to other communicators about what they experienced when they connected with different animals. I enrolled in Joanne's Mentoring Programme and, as a result, successfully established my animal communication business. And yet, I still held this block that I couldn't talk to my own dog.

Now I live with Maja, who came to me nearly a year ago at five years of age. She has shown me that I only have to think about going on a walk and she starts getting excited. I don't say anything out loud or make any actions to give her a physical clue, but she runs around looking at me expectantly. This tells me we have a connection whereby she can certainly receive communication, more than just relying on verbal cues or body language.

I wished I could have the same level of communication with Maja as I do with my client's pets. By this, I mean having conversations that come through as words in my mind as well as the sensory signs of visuals, sounds, smells, tastes, emotions and sensations.

I know I'm able to speak the language of pets when helping pet parents, yet with Maja I'm often lost for what to ask her, or it seems that I'm receiving very little from her. When Joanne announced she was looking for communicators to participate in a communication session about this struggle I was experiencing with Maja, I jumped at the chance!

When the session started, Joanne said Maja was asking me about the difference I experience when I communicate with other people's pets, compared to communicating with her. Maja often looks at me and I just know she wants to tell me something, but I don't know what. Sometimes I think it's more difficult when she's there physically. It's easier when I connect with her when we're not in the same room, using my mind and focusing on bringing her energy near me. But even then, I'm questioning the information that comes through and wondering if I'm making everything up.

One of the specific things I wanted to be able to share with Maja was that she is welcome to sleep on our bed – my husband and I would love her to sleep on it with us! She comes up in the evening and gets a biscuit, then she lies down and sometimes sleeps, but then suddenly wakes up as if something has startled her and immediately jumps off the bed. Her body language suggests that she feels she's not meant to be there.

We've tried to tell her it's okay, that we love her and want her there, but it makes no difference. I keep wondering if she's actually jumping off because she thinks she's not allowed on the bed, or whether she's made an instant decision to get off because it's what she wants to do. I feel if we could actually communicate, then I wouldn't have to second guess.

Joanne said Maja isn't a chatterbox, but she wants to have what she terms 'a loving communication'. She shared that she feels so fortunate to be living with me, and to have the added bonus of being able to share communications, as opposed to living a life with someone else and having a 'normal dog life'. I knew she appreciated me being a communicator. I believe deep down she would like to play a part in helping me in the healing work I offer in my animal communication business, but I hadn't yet been able to connect with her to find out how this could be put into practice.

Joanne sensed with Maja that she may be more relaxed and open to having conversations when she's outdoors. This surprised me somewhat, for what I've observed with Maja's behaviour is that she is less attentive to me when we're outdoors. This made me realise that often what we see is not what is going on for our pets, and I needed to keep an open mind. In other words, just because Maja doesn't come when I call her when outdoors doesn't necessarily mean she'll be less attentive when we're communicating using the sensory signs.

On the topic of the bed scenario, Maja communicated that she would like more humour to be used in such a situation, and for me to be light-hearted towards her reaction, rather than take it seriously. This way the energy of the humour will invite her back onto the bed, rather than for me to project my concern, thinking she felt as if she'd done something she shouldn't have.

Maja also told Joanne she doesn't want me to take myself so seriously either. She'd love it if when I feel like I've not done something, have done something wrong or something goes wrong, I can show her that I can laugh about it. That's the energy she wants to bring into her family. I couldn't deny this was good advice from Maja, and was applicable to me! Overall, Maja has asked if I could fill our home with more laughter.

In fact, Maja had been making Joanne laugh throughout the session, and she said I just needed to allow her to share some humour with me. She said she was excited to start conversations and suggested I could ask her to share with me a humorous way to look at different situations and allow her to suggest the best way to do it. I thought this was a great idea! She told Joanne that laughter is our communication bond and humour is the key to unlocking conversations. She said when there are problems in life, it's humour that gets you through.

I wasn't expecting what came up in the session with Joanne, because Maja always looks so serious! So when she said to look on the bright side of life and look at things with humour, I did wonder if Joanne was actually talking to my dog! Once again, it reminded me that people don't always reflect their true character by their appearance. The saying 'Don't judge a book by its cover' comes to mind.

Reflecting on the session, I remembered there have been times we've felt like there's something in Maja that is light-hearted and wants to have fun. I was excited to think this could be the key to opening up my communication with her, and also for helping her to express herself more freely.

Since the session with Joanne, I've been implementing the things Maja suggested and it appears to be working. We're having lots more fun and playing and laughing together more.

She still gets off the bed, and as much as we would love for her to be there, we've accepted that she's spontaneous and lives in the moment. She is deciding that she doesn't want to be on the bed any longer and wants her own space. Maybe her dog bed is just too comfy! We're not worried about it anymore, because we know she doesn't do it because she thinks she's not allowed to be with us.

WHAT MAJA HAD TO SAY:

I know my mum has had a tough time with her previous dog, so I'm not expecting her to bring humour into everything. However, knowing she listened to me and is open to my suggestions, I just love her even more.

For her to want to know what I want and consider something so unusual, that's what makes me feel so happy. As much as she likes things to be clear or expected, she's also very open to different things. She just goes with the idea and tries it out.

Intention: HUMOUR

Communication Exercise:

- Get hold of a comic book. Yes! You can get these online too.
- As you read the funny stories, relay them to your pet, using your imagination to send the pictures, words, sound effects and emotions to them and share in the laughter together!
- Make humour the focus in your relationship with your pet.
- Take time to engage in activities you both enjoy and use communication to recall what you did together.

SENSORY SIGNS: VISUAL, SOUND, EMOTION, SENSATION

Take a few moments to pause here and journal your experience.

CHAPTER 19

Love

Belinda and her Male Dog, Blaze

Here we have an unexpected communication revelation. Blaze displayed the need for constant attention using physical behaviours and verbal cues. Movement and voice were Blaze's way of declaring, 'I'm not heard!' Yet Belinda thought the opposite, for she always responded to his display for needing attention.

Blaze's continued desire to show his true feelings was likened to a Romeo and Juliet story, along with the visual of Blaze dressed in a tuxedo with a rose held between his teeth, depicting the love he knew Belinda would understand but which she had long shut away. He needed to connect to that depth of emotion so they could each tap into that ocean of deep love. And therein lies their safe place – their emotional sanctuary.

WHAT BELINDA HAD TO SAY:

I originally became interested in animal communication to help Blaze. I got him at eight weeks of age, and to me he was the perfect puppy. I remember the feeling of connection the moment I saw him, and thereafter he was my little shadow. At six months of age his behaviour changed. He grew nervous and was uncomfortable around other people and dogs. I began to worry about him. Taking Blaze for walks, or to see the vets, became very challenging. I remember wishing that I knew what he was thinking. I just wanted to know why he was reacting in this way. I researched all the available training techniques to see how I could help him. People would comment to me that I had a reactive dog, but deep down I knew he was misunderstood.

I also decided to explore energy healing and communication to see if this could help him. I then spent the next seven years attending training classes and studied numerous holistic practices including Reiki, crystal healing and essential oils. I was so glad I didn't give up on him, because all the things I was learning started to help him, slowly but surely.

Even though we've been through many challenges together, I still felt like I couldn't communicate with him. I'd tell him out loud what I wanted from him, and although he'd respond by showing me he was listening and doing what I told him, I never received a reply in the way I expected so I would know he received my message. Instead, he'd look at me as if to say, 'Are you not listening?'

I just couldn't move past his physical behaviour to quieten my mind enough to access the sensory signs of visual, sound, smell, taste, emotion and sensation to receive his communication. I tried using a photograph to connect while he was in another room, so as not to be physically distracted by his presence, but then he'd come to find me. He'd fetch me a toy to throw and that would distract me!

I was frustrated. I could communicate with other people's pets, but struggled with Blaze. I seemed to have convinced myself I was making it up because I know Blaze. When Joanne announced in her Community Group that she was interested in exploring with communicators how they would like to improve their communication with their own pets, I was delighted to take part with Blaze.

As I sat down to start the session with Joanne, Blaze was jumping around and barking. I tried to tell him to lie down and be quiet, but Joanne told me to just leave him and let him do whatever he wanted to do. She said he was so happy about the communication, and she was enjoying his energy. He was telling her that he loves me so much and is so proud to be with me, and for me to be his mum. She said each time he was barking he was shouting out phrases like, 'I love my Mum,' or, 'Look, we're together!'

Joanne then asked if I was able to bypass the barking and jumping around Blaze was doing, and focus on connecting with the emotion underlying this display of behaviour. Although it felt challenging to avoid being distracted by Blaze, I followed Joanne's instructions and received the sensory sign of emotion to be 'excitement'.

Joanne then explained to Blaze that humans are easily distracted by movement, noise and sound, and it was quite challenging for me to go beyond that, because that's where my attention goes to. The fact that he's running around, barking and forcing himself into my personal space, makes it difficult for me. She also told him that as lovely as this physical display is, he's trying too hard. Blaze told Joanne the reason he's being so physical all the time is because he feels like I don't actually get how much he loves me.

Joanne then questioned whether he was right, whether I did know how much he loved me. I believed I did, because I knew we had a very good bond, but Joanne said that wasn't enough for

Blaze. Joanne explained that if his love was measured on a scale from one to ten, he was at level ten (highest), but I'm only aware of it at around level four. He wants me to experience every level of it, so he has another six levels to tell me about – and the only way to tell me is to be in my face, because he says I'm not getting it.

Joanne offered an analogy of a person who loves eating chocolates, but when they try to share this with someone who isn't interested in eating chocolate, that person cannot connect with that desire. This was how Blaze felt about what he was trying to share with me. Because of this, he was being forced to continue to communicate in a very physical way. All he wanted was for me to dive deep enough to feel every level of love he has for me, then the communication lines would open and flow, which is also something he would like.

Thinking about it, I realised the only time I did really feel like that was when my children were born. Although I love my dogs, it's a different type of love – the type you feel for your best friend, or maybe even your parents, so I just needed to go deeper.

Blaze shared that there are times in people's lives when they may have felt this type of love but have also felt deep hurt or grief, so they've shut off that level of love. They then start to fear feeling that level of love again because the pain of loss, grief or rejection could be greater, so they shut the love off and don't allow themselves to feel it, or they tone it down. He said his suggestion isn't for me to go back and relive those memories if I have them, he was just saying that he was missing that level of understanding or connection, and that is what he would like to share with me. When I am able to connect with that deep love, he won't need to make such a show of it. He would like not to have to keep giving me this physical show of love all of the time.

Blaze's suggestion was for me to journal or think about an experience in my life where I have felt such deep love for someone else. Joanne said Blaze wasn't asking me to think about the deepest love I'd felt for an animal. This had to be a time when I'd felt the deepest love I could feel for another being. I had to get as personal as possible, like when you're a teenager and you have your first love, then you're completely crushed when it doesn't work out. It had to have that sort of intensity, like when you watch a romantic film and are drawn into how much the characters love each other and can't live without each other. Blaze wanted me to connect with that feeling, that emotion and experience, then really understand that this is how he feels about me. His life depends on me, he couldn't live without me, and I mean the world to him.

Joanne said our animals bring us healing, so for me to tap into that emotion was going to be very healing for me. She suggested I watch love films with Blaze. Interestingly, I don't enjoy watching love films, preferring comedy and sci-fi. I wondered, was there a link with not wanting to consciously connect with that emotion? However, Joanne said this was for a purpose. It wasn't about changing my interests, but to tap into what was important for Blaze.

It made sense. I understood, but was doubting it. I did what Joanne suggested though, and watched a few films with Blaze. Normally, he likes to be on his own and wouldn't be downstairs with me while I sit watching television, but he actually came and sat beside me while I watched the films. He licked the tears off my face and pawed at me when I became emotional.

Since the communication session with Joanne, my relationship with Blaze has definitely improved. I now have the understanding around how much he loves me and he's a lot calmer. I feel this could also be because a shift has occurred in me. I couldn't open myself up before because I've had a lot of trauma in my life. Blaze has helped me to open up emotionally, whereas before I was a bit shut down.

WHAT BLAZE HAD TO SAY:

I know my mum loves me, and she knows it wasn't about me believing that she thought I didn't love her. It was about her understanding the depth of love I have for her. It's wonderful she made the effort to sit and watch soppy films and have sofa time with me. That means the world to me, so I want her to keep doing that.

There's something I know about her that I'm going to keep between me and her, but it's something to do with the heart and depth of love, and I want her to continue working on that as well. I really do appreciate her opening up her depth of emotion so I can tell her how much I love her, and she can genuinely say, 'I know.'

Intention: LOVE

Communication Exercise:
- Draw a heart shape.
- Write in the middle the name of your pet.
- Place one hand over the heart drawing and your other hand on your heart area.
- Close your eyes and bring your attention to your heartbeat. Stay with the rhythm of your heart for a while, until you feel your body and mind begin to relax as the sound of your heartbeat gets louder and the sensation of your heartbeat deeper.
- On your next breath, breathe out the love from your heart down along the arm of the hand placed on your heart drawing that holds your pet's name.
- Breathe this pure energy of love into the drawing, sending the love to your pet.
- On your next breath, breathe in the love from the heart drawing, from your pet, up along your arm and into your heart. Allow the other hand that is placed on your heart area to feel this love entering your heart space.

SENSORY SIGNS: EMOTION, VISUAL, SENSATION

Take a few moments to pause here and journal your experience.

CHAPTER 20

Relax – Focus – Communicate

Let's look at ways you can create the ultimate setting for you and your pets to feel comfortable so conversations flow easily. Why is it important that you are at ease while you communicate? Because often when animals are stressed, or you are stressed or distracted, you won't be open to listening.

I used to think that in order to be able to communicate with my pets I had to be still. Still my mind. Still my body. To a degree that is true, I do need to be free of distraction. It's important I am relaxed, yet focused, but it isn't always necessary to be in a meditative state.

Your environment plays an important part in supporting your communication time with your pets. Taking a stroll in nature or relaxing at home can be a good time to have a conversation. Ideally, you are not distracted and your state of mind is focused and clear.

You can also use dreamtime. When it comes to remembering your dreams, you want to be intentional.

- Set the intention to remember your dreams.
- Keep a notebook on your bedside table.
- Upon waking, the moment you wake, just before you're completely fully alert and you have that sense of what you might have dreamt about, write the dream in your notebook.

Often, with my pets from the past who have passed and now are in the spirit world, I find their visitations in my dreams very comforting.

You don't have to be physically with your pets when you're communicating with them. Distance communication is something I'd like you to explore, as there will be times the distance helps with the objectivity, particularly if you're wanting to talk about more difficult and sensitive issues when your own feelings are heightened.

Sometimes it's actually better to communicate with them when they're not sitting in front of you or staring at you. Otherwise, your tendency will be to shift into observational mode, looking for signs, seeking some evidence straight away. You may want to know that what you're thinking and asking them is going to work. So, you test it out by saying, 'Go on. Show me you can hear me by moving your right paw.' Then you wait to see if they do it. If they don't, you'll be thinking, 'Oh no, it's not working.'

I will tell you – your pets do hear you. 'Move your right paw,' you say, but they may be thinking, 'Why? What for?' So you might not see it, and that could be the reason!

Start with something light-hearted when beginning the communication, even if you're really worried about something. You want to make sure you don't only choose to communicate with your pet when it's something serious, so explore communication with your pets about easy topics, perhaps sharing about something you've done earlier.

Often, I'll say to my pets, 'There's something I really need to talk to you about, but let's just start off with something that's pleasant for both you and me.' My Mitch often enjoys going over what happened in his walks as an opening conversation. This boy loves sniffing, so he is eager to share his experience of the scents and sensations he gets from being outdoors. After a few moments of listening to him, we can then move on to the topic of conversation I had in mind.

From my example, you can choose an activity that your pet enjoys. And remember, their experience may be what you already perceive, or it may be surprising to you, so don't fall into the trap of making assumptions. For example, you might think to yourself, 'Oh, my dog likes to play ball. She plays ball all the time.' Your dog may play with her ball a lot, but pause for a moment and consider that you won't know how she experiences it *from her perspective*.

Believe me when I tell you that although it's one activity that is the topic of conversation, on the surface at least (such as, your dog likes to play with the ball), when your dog communicates about it, the conversation can be in depth, as your dog may have a lot to say about something she is excited about!

And it's good to remember not to immediately rely on the human language, and instead become familiar with using the sensory signs, which is the form of language your pet uses.

To ask your pet about an activity they enjoy, say to them, 'I want to be able to experience it from your perspective. I want to experience your emotions. I want to receive your thoughts. I want to physically sense what you feel. I want to connect with your memories. I want to smell and taste as you would.'

That is a real conversation for your pets to engage with you about!

When you're at the beginning stages, you may feel it's clumsy or slow – that's because you're used to talking using words. The key is not to be disheartened.

You may expect to 'hear' conversations right here, right now, but whenever you get a feeling, smell, taste or a memory, I want you to be excited about it! It's a matter of recognising what you are receiving.

It's now time for you to give it a go!

CHAPTER 21

Steps to Success

First – Imagination

First, activate your imagination!

As a child, did you use imagination to have a good time? I spent hours daydreaming in school lessons, taking myself off to faraway places, living a life as a princess or a ballerina. At home, I held imaginary tea parties with teddy bears and dolls. I even had adventures in my mind of battles involving superheroes, where the good always won over the bad!

Let's consider the underlying messages we hold about using our imagination. Interesting how as adults most of us will have stopped daydreaming. We might consider it a waste of time and tell ourselves we must 'live in the real world' instead, while beginning to believe imagination is not a positive ability.

Yet visual artists, creative designers, inventors, architects and photographers are examples of professionals who use imagination to their advantage. I believe imagination allows us to explore solutions to problems, change our perspectives, and even recreate past experiences. In short, imagination gives us limitless access to our potential!

Through activating your imagination, you are going to connect with the sensory signs your pets use to communicate. When you recognise the sensory signs and how to use them, receiving information from your pet, and giving information to them, is far easier.

Imagination Exercise

Begin by imagining yourself in a busy, crowded place. I want you to imagine the scene.

- What can you see around you? Is there something in particular that catches your eye?
- Fully immerse yourself into allowing your imagination to bring information to you. Can you zoom in closer and see how much more detail you can get?
- Now imagine the sounds coming from this busy and crowded place. What sounds can you imagine you would hear?
- Allow your attention to be drawn to a particular sound that catches your attention. Imagine the sound getting louder and louder until it drowns out the other sounds and noises.
- Now imagine you come across a café. You walk in, greeted by the smells from the café.
- What smells come to you? Be as imaginative as you like!
- Now imagine sipping a drink you've just bought. Taste it. Using your imagination, allow the experience of sipping the drink to be as real as you can allow it to be.

- Now walk out of the café and imagine having to cross a very busy road. What emotions do you feel?
- Using your imagination, create the scene of crossing this very busy road and being in touch with how your body feels.
- As you start to cross the road, what sensations is your body experiencing?
- Now imagine yourself making the decision that it's time to leave this crowded, busy place.
- Imagine how you feel about arriving home and what you can expect, what you know will be there for you when you arrive.

How did you experience the visuals, sounds, smells, tastes, emotions, sensations and knowingness? This will be similar to how you'll experience receiving the sensory signs when communicating with your pet. You'll find that some sensory signs are stronger than others and, in time, the more you activate your imagination and connect with all the sensory signs, the more you'll develop your ability to send and receive information from your pet.

Often, when we say we want to communicate with our pets, our expectation is that we'll hear it as words, sentences or phrases as we would with another person. However is this the only way communication comes through from them? Imagine you and your pet share a special telephone line – it's special because you communicate without words. As humans, we depend so much on words that, if we take away words, we can be quite lost. But you and I know, too, that without words we can still communicate using the sensory signs of visuals, sounds, smells, taste, emotions, physical sensations and knowingness.

It's also important to understand that you and your pet have free will. Either of you can initiate the phone call, and either can choose whether to answer the call or not in that moment! I always have a little chuckle about this, because often I'll say to Donny I've 'dialled a call to him' and asked a question, only to wait and not receive any response immediately.

Then I think, 'Let me try another way.' I ask him another question, then I think, 'He's not saying anything,' quickly followed by, 'Why isn't he answering me?' And on it goes. My doubts kick in, leading to frustration.

Then it struck me – it's similar to when I send someone a text message, and then I keep checking it, wondering why there isn't an immediate reply. My thoughts range from questioning whether the text has been delivered, to believing the person doesn't want to speak to me! It dawned on me that Donny's communication style is that he likes to answer my questions *in his own time.*

That's how I learnt with Donny that it's for me to ask a question and leave it. I found that, often, when I'm not thinking about it and I'm doing something else, his answer can come to me. Mind you, I have to be aware it's him answering me and have my awareness of the sensory signs coming in, otherwise I'll miss it. That's exactly what happened in the first couple of years when I was trying to learn how to communicate with him, thinking he didn't want to communicate with me, or that I wasn't doing it right.

On the other hand, another of my dogs, Mhyah, is just so expressive. She loves conversing. In fact, she almost can't stop telling me what she needs, so it's very different with her. And because of that, I can adjust and adapt to her communication style.

Second – Intuition

Secondly, be intuitive with your approach.

Knowing animals are naturally instinctive and intuitive, it was clear that I needed to develop this aspect within myself. It follows that the more intuitive I become, the easier it is to connect with my pets. Even so, it wasn't a straightforward journey for me, in the sense that although I seek to live intuitively, I didn't always understand fully how to 'be intuitive'.

So began my journey of discovering how to explore and deepen my intuition, a journey that led me in many different directions. In the practice of communicating with your pet, being intuitive simply means to be in a state where your conscious mind takes a back seat, allowing your subconscious mind to come to the forefront so you are highly receptive to the sensory signs presented to you. By being intuitive with your approach, you can easily tune into the same frequency as your pets.

Here's a fun exercise!

I want you to imagine being your pet. I want you to connect with what it's like to be them.

What is it like to experience the world through their senses, connecting with their visuals, sounds, smells, tastes, emotions and their physical sensations?

- When they're eating their dinner, connect and ask your pet to share what's going on inside their mouth. What does the texture of their food feel like?
- Do this mindfully.
- Close your eyes so you focus inwards.
- Slow the whole experience down.
- Even though they look as if they're wolfing the food down, pause in that moment and ask your pet, 'How does it feel going down your throat? What was that like? What was the smell like? What's your experience of it going down into your stomach and your digestion?'
- Communication is an inner experience – to 'be' them.

Third – Insight

Thirdly, be open to receiving insights.

Insight is an experience of a sudden and clear shift in perception, a breakthrough that occurs from gaining an understanding of another, perhaps even profound thoughts that enter your mind without your conscious thinking.

This has been the game changer in the relationship I share with Donny, Ziggi, Mhyah and Mitch since discovering animal communication. I assumed the roles of owner and parent when Donny and Mitch came into my life. I made all the decisions for them, from the food they ate and where we went for our walks, to major changes such as new jobs I took on and home relocations. It never occurred to me that my pets would have their own views and feelings and would appreciate being part of the decision-making.

Now we're able to communicate with one another, I often hold family conferences so we can each express honestly what may and what may not be working well in our relationship. The information they send me when I seek their opinions, feelings, thoughts and views enters my mind in a way that allows me intuitively to comprehend the true meaning.

Ziggi is particularly communicative when it comes to my work as an animal communicator. He'll initiate ideas, projects and plans for spreading the word about animal communication. Often my best work has been the result of an inspired insight from this wonder cat!

Are you ready to uncover what your pets can tell you?

Get started with my free *Roadmap To Mastering Animal Communication with your Pet*, type this address below into your web browser: animalcommunicationinsights.com/roadmap/

CHAPTER 22

Transform Your Relationship

Although I didn't have the opportunity to have a pet in my adult life until my late forties, I had longed for the companionship and unconditional love I experienced as a young child with my dog, Lassie. I was a lonely child, and Lassie became my constant companion. When I arrived home from school every day to an empty house, Lassie would be there for me without fail. I remember telling her everything, and I absolutely believed she understood every word. I even tried to teach her to say the word 'hello' by moving her mouth with my hands, and often said to her, 'I wish you could talk.'

All these years later, I know in my heart Lassie absolutely knew all that I confided in her, and that, as a child, I believed I knew what Lassie was thinking and feeling from the Imagined Information I received.

Through the twists and turns of life, I embarked on a path of holistic therapy practices and energy healing work, which then led me to exploring working with oracle cards – and that's where the story comes full circle and how my connection with Isabelle came about.

Since the day Donny came into my life, he's been the instigator for me to leave mainstream employment to pursue the entrepreneurial route. Mitch, Ziggi and Mhyah joined the family soon after, each bringing me incredible wisdom and guidance because I've learnt to listen to them.

Our pets would love to know they can guide us, offer their views and share their wisdom. As their human companions, this may not be obvious to us as we take on the immediate role of parent, guardian and caretaker by making decisions for them, and even trying to fix their issues.

My wish is for your eyes to open to how communications from your pets come through.

I wholeheartedly encourage you to learn the language of your pets. I hope you get excited about what animal communication can facilitate in strengthening the bond even more between you and your pets.

When your communications with your pets begin to flow, I know your relationship with them will be transformed!

About the Author

Founder of Animal Communication Insights, Joanne is an animal (interspecies) communicator and mentor. Joanne's business is twofold. Firstly, she supports pet parents who want to understand how their pets are feeling and what they need (no more second guessing!), so a positive resolution can be achieved with ease for everyone in the family.

Joanne also mentors professional animal communicators who want to create a successful business doing what they love.

Joanne is available for consultations, teaching and guest speaking.

Keep in touch with Joanne when you sign up for the free *Roadmap To Mastering Animal Communication with your Pet.* Type the address below into your browser:

animalcommunicationinsights.com/roadmap

Acknowledgements

Heartfelt thanks to the communicators and their animal counterparts for taking part, and to Abbie for her paintings that perceptibly capture the character of the animals, bringing forth their presence as we connect with their stories.

Without a doubt, the biggest thanks go to Donny, Ziggi, Mhyah and Mitch, my pet family. To them, I say, 'Where do I begin to tell you how you've enriched my life? You have loved me like no one has ever loved me. You have forgiven me like no one has ever forgiven me. You stand by me, you believe in me and you listen to me.'

For you, the reader and loving pet parent, this book exists to serve you. Thank you for allowing me to share with you my belief that when you learn animal communication, richer, deeper and truly enlightening conversations can take place between you and your pets!

In Honour of Pets Who Have Passed

Since the writing of this book began, Gamera, Tiger, Skyla and Ronda have left their earthly bodies and taken on a new energy in the realm of what is known as the afterlife, or spirit dimension. I am grateful to have their stories to pass on.

Glossary

Animal Communication – applicable to all animals, domestic and wild. Synonymous with Interspecies Communication and Pet Communication.

Chakra – refers to energy points in the body.

Community Group – Facebook membership group run by Joanne for pet parents and animal communicators.

Communication Session – whereby Joanne gathered the twelve communicators and their nominated pets with the view to finding out from the pets how they can improve their communications together. Beginning in December 2020, Joanne met with each communicator via video link and connected with their pet using a photo. Joanne held a 60-minute session, communicating with the pet and sharing the information live with the communicator.

Imagined Information – refers to the non-physical information Joanne receives when connecting with telepathic, energetic, intuitive messages.

Pet/Companion – animal, domestic animal companion.

Pet owner/Pet parent – human companion, guardian, caretaker.

Sensory Signs – the use of intuitive senses in animal communication: visual, sound, smell, taste, emotion, physical sensation and knowing.

Toroidal Field – exists around all matter – humans, animals, trees, all living beings and even inanimate objects. Most torus dynamics contain two toruses, or 'tori'. One spirals upwards and the other downwards.

Resources

Animal Communication Insights – **Joanne Yeoh**
animalcommunicationinsights.com

Soul Coaching Oracle Card Certification Programme
– Denise Linn
deniselinnseminars.com

Speak! Good Human – **Josh Coen**
talktoanimals.weebly.com

Animal Communicators
Featured

(in order of appearance)

Annette Norbury
Founder of Annette Norbury Animal Communication.
facebook.com/Annette-Norbury-Founder-of-Annette-Norbury-Animal-Communications-101136985382161

Becky Shuttleworth
Founder of Therapy for Dogs.
therapy-4-dogs.com

Cheri Hayashi
Animal Communicator, Pet Medium & Founder of Sakura
Spiritual Academy.
cherimichelle.com
sakuraspiritualacademy.com

Emilie Yegikyan
Pet parent and caretaker to sixteen cats – six indoors and ten
outdoors.
(Using animal communication to help keep a harmonious
relationship between all of my cats.)

Tracey Doolan
Pet parent to two Labrador dogs, Sandy and Casey.
(Offering animal communication to help friends, family and my
dogs, as well as energy healing.)

Jason Wickens
Reiki energy healer and practitioner.
talkingtoanimals.co.uk

Piedad Gracia Santolaria
Founder of Animals Talk, Intuitive Communications.
animalsandhumansintuitivecommunicator.wordpress.com

Judith Hurst
Communicator working with Spirit Guides for Soul Healing.
JudithHurst.com

Verena Debnar
Living a Magic Life with Transformative Animal & Nature
Communication through Energy Alchemy.

Debbie Watson
Energy healing for people and pets.
thegentlevibe.com

Tanja Gauer
Animal Intuitive – Communicator and Healer.
tanjagauer.com

Belinda Eaton
Founder of Animal and Companion Reiki. Energy healing for
reactive dogs.

Paintings

Abbie Withers
Animal Portrait Artist capturing the character of the animal.
Founder of Beyond Words Animal Communicator & Medium.
beyond-words.co.uk